WWW.TThGLNNGTI of (W --11A)
RGF : MLSA Sl

C000143448

RGF MLSA 7438 350 ... T
£113,273
(00 34) 952 850016

Going to Live on the Costa del Sol

PROPERTY LETTING FOR SPANISH
                                    NON - RESIDENTS
A NON - RESIDENT
IS TAXED IN SPAIN ON INCOME
ARISING FROM SPANISH PROPERTY AT
THG RATE OF 25% ON GROSS INCOME
WITHOUT ANY DEDUCTIONS OF EXPENSES
OF INTEREST COSTS.
    IT IS THG TENANT WHO HAS A
OBLIGATION TO FILE A TAX RETURN 6
TO PAY THE 25% TO THG HACIENDA
                            (TAX OFFICE)
THG LANDLORD MUST ASK FOR A COPY
OF THIS RETURN IN ORDER TO PROVE
THAT THG TAX HAS BEEN PAID, AND IT
WILL BE REQUIRED AS EVIDENCE OF OVERSEAS
TAX PAID FOR ANY DOUBLE TAX CLAIM

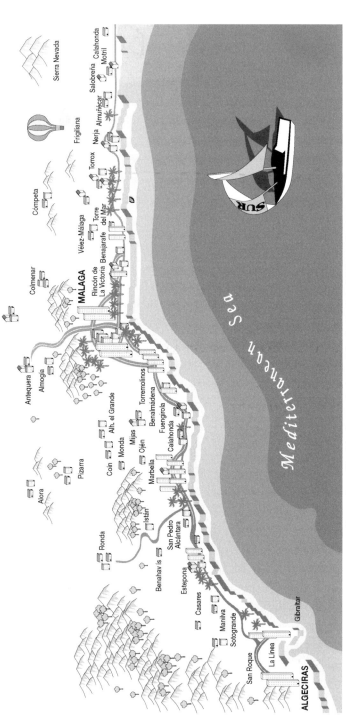

Reproduced by kind permission of *Sur in English*, Malaga, Spain.

WWW. OLARY. COM
ROF: 12357 £155-00 EUROS
   3 BED - + POOL (communal)
ROF 15896 €3 BED £159.00 euros
ROF 16760 ← 3 BED £ 165 euros

Going to Live on the Costa del Sol

A practical guide to a new life

Tom Provan

OFICA GSTEBNA
CN 340 km 166
URBANIZACION
  BEL AIR
29680
  ESTEPONA
TEL (84)
  95 288 7119

TOWNHOUSE
3 BED   135 m²

SAN PEDRO -
  GSTEPONA
£184 EUROS

ROF:
13701

OR

RCF 1G1B
3 BED TOWNHOUSE
      95 m²

Published by How To Books Ltd,
3 Newtec Place, Magdalen Road,
Oxford OX4 1RE. United Kingdom.
Tel: (01865) 793806. Fax: (01865) 248780
email: info@howtobooks.co.uk
www.howtobooks.co.uk

British Library Cataloguing in Publication Data.
A catalogue record for this book is available from the British Library.

Produced for How To Books by Deer Park Productions, Tavistock
Cover design by Baseline Arts Ltd, Oxford
Typesetting and design by Sparks – www.sparks.co.uk
Printed and bound in Great Britain by Cromwell Press, Trowbridge, Wiltshire
Illustrations by Nickie Averill

NOTE: The material contained in this book is set out in good faith for general guidance and no liability can be accepted for loss or expense incurred as a result of relying in particular circumstances on statements made in this book. Laws and regulations are complex and liable to change, and readers should check the current position with the relevant authorities before making personal arrangements.

Contents

List of Tables

Acknowledgements

In the preparation of this book I would like to thank my many friends both in Spain and in the UK who helped me to fill in the gaps in my own knowledge of life on the Costa del Sol, and who were prepared to read the manuscript and check it for accuracy and honesty. I would like especially to acknowledge Mercedes Enriques de Salamanca, who has provided invaluable assistance in checking the manuscript for accuracy with respect to local information.

There are many other books that have been written about moving to – and living in – Spain. These, and the weekly editorials of the local English language newspapers, have also been a valuable source of information. Many of these books and newspapers are listed in the sources of further information (Appendix 8).

Many thanks to Nikki Read of How To Books for the confidence she showed in me to actually ask for this book to be written following the publication of my first book *Gone to Spain*. Thanks also to the staff of How To Books, the editor and Deer Park Productions – who put the book together – for their dedication and professionalism in providing books that help individuals to make life-changing decisions.

Lastly, I'd like to acknowledge the encouragement and support of my partner, Julian, who has had to endure the frustrations of computers crashing, the days when inspiration did not exist, and all the other frustrations which occur when a book is being prepared.

Special note

The information contained in this book is provided in good faith and drawn from the experiences of people who already live on the Costa del Sol. It has been checked for accuracy, but neither the author nor the publisher can be held responsible for decisions made as a result of reading this book. Anyone contemplating a permanent move to the Costa del Sol should appoint their own impartial advisors to guide them through all aspects of the move. Laws and regulations change constantly.

1 Introduction

The Costa del Sol is now one of the favourite destinations for the British choosing to relocate to the sun and enjoy a better quality of life. Reality TV programmes regularly feature property in the southern regions of Spain, although the nature of such programmes means that they cannot answer all the questions that potential relocators might want to ask. In fact, they generally only feature the positive points. This book deals with the positives and the negatives.

Property prices

Property is still relatively inexpensive compared to many parts of the UK and the overall cost of living is definitely much lower. Property prices have been rising dramatically over the last few years and in some areas have more than doubled in the last two to three years. The Costa del Sol is now one of Europe's boom areas. This is potentially positive for long-term investment. In fact, the region is often referred to as the California of Europe. It would be wonderful to be able to insert a table here to tell you what you could buy for €200,000 but unfortunately by the time this book is printed the information would probably be out of date.

Suffice to say that the first property we bought here was a two bedroom/one bathroom apartment with good views which cost €90k in January 2001 and sold for €162k in September 2003.

Lifestyle

The climate is definitely better and the overall quality and pace of life is much more pleasant. There are many British people who have settled here who are working hard and providing a good lifestyle for themselves and their families. Healthcare is better and much cheaper in real terms. There are good schools for families with young children.

How many Brits live on the Costa del Sol?

This question is almost impossible to answer with any real degree of accuracy. Depending on the source the figures differ. The official census of the province of Malaga reports over 70,000 foreign residents. In this figure there are many British residents but this figure only reports those who have actually bothered to register with the authorities. If new arrivals do not register, they will not be counted.

There are other figures, which report that there are already 1.2 million British homeowners in Spain with a further 600,000 planning to buy a second home here in the next five years. Within this figure there are many living in Malaga and Cadiz provinces. Whatever figure you accept there are a lot of British residents already here, and many planning to relocate in the future.

It is interesting to note, also, that whereas in the past most Brits relocating to the Costa del Sol were retiring to Spain to live in the sun, the Ministry of the Interior in Malaga now reports that the average age of the foreign residents in the province is 45 and has been dropping very fast during the last few years. More and more people are choosing to leave the UK and actually work and bring up their families in an environment that is potentially much better.

This in itself raises many more questions. It is one thing to retire or semi-retire to the sun but it is much more difficult to decide to relocate your family from one country to another in order to build a new life. I hope you will find the answers to most of your questions in the following pages. Not only is the Costa del Sol potentially a wonderful place to live – it is also potentially a wonderful place in which to bring up your family.

Summary

First ask yourself 'what type of resident will I be?'

I want to move permanently to Spain

For anyone planning a move from the UK to Spain who has plans to sell up totally in the UK, the considerations differ according to age, family situation and long-term plans. It is vital that you know all the answers to all the questions relating to work, tax, healthcare, educating your children and, even if you are young, the pension situation in Spain. When you reach pensionable age you need to know that you will be provided for.

In planning a permanent move it is even more important to choose the right property from the outset. If you have any doubts at all, rent first. Then you will know that your chosen area is the right place for you and your family. If you need to sell the first property you buy here the estate agent will take 5% in commission and, before you are officially resident, another 5% will be withheld from your sale price against any capital gains tax (legally, the capital gains tax is 35% of the rise in value). Whatever your sales price, 10% has immediately disappeared from your pocket.

I want to move permanently to Spain and I have a family

First thing, check out local schools and the immediate availability of places before you commit yourself to any property no matter how wonderful it appears to be. The school run could be several kilometres and this will be five days a week during term time unless there is a local school bus.

You also need to consider whether you want your children to go to a local state school where they will need to learn Spanish, or do you have – or will you have – the funds to pay for private education in an international school where education will be in English?

You must realise that if your children go to a local Spanish school they may initially be at a disadvantage if they do not speak Spanish, and they might lose up to a year of their education before they are fluent in the language. But, please remember, children learn very quickly and in the longer term they might benefit – they should leave the Spanish state school system totally bilingual. Remember too that after English, Spanish is the most widely spoken language in the world, so fluent Spanish could be an advantage in any future career that your children might wish to follow.

With children you also need to consider the local availability of recreational facilities.

- Where is the nearest cinema and do they show films in English?

- Where can I buy computer games (most modern kids love them)?

- What sports facilities are available within easy travelling distance?

- Where will my children's friends live? Will this be a problem in terms of travelling time? It will not be a problem for your children but it could be for you.

I want to work in Spain

There is a lot of work in Spain if you want or need to work. If you speak fluent Spanish you can apply for many of the positions that are advertised in the English language press here, and you will have a good chance of finding well paid work that will keep you occupied. If your Spanish is fluent then, of course, under EU rules you can apply for any job in full competition with the local population.

If you do not speak fluent Spanish the possibilities are more limited; but they do exist. We know many people who make a very respectable living in jobs that cater solely for the expatriate community. Possible work opportunities are dealt with at greater length in a future chapter. We also know many people who run their own businesses, some of which are totally geared to the expatriate community – more of this later.

Working for a Spanish-registered company will, of course, mean that you will need to contribute to Spanish social security and thus gain the benefits from this.

If you choose to live in the western end of the Costa del Sol you could also look for work in Gibraltar. Spanish would not be so necessary and you would then have Gibraltar social security to support you and possibly also your family.

I propose to retire to Spain

If you fall into this category there are two possible questions that must be asked. Do your retirement plans mean that you will spend 12 months of the year in your new home in Spain or do you propose to spend winters in Spain and summers in the UK? If you only spend six months of the year in Spain your tax situation and your legal status will be very different. This is also dealt with later in the book.

If you fall into this category your choice of suitable property may also be different.

2 The Costa del Sol

According to some guidebooks, the Costa del Sol stretches from Almunecar to Tarifa and comprises the entire coastline of Malaga province together with part of Cadiz province.

Officially the Costa del Sol is the coastline of Malaga province – Nerja to Manilva. This is the boom coast of southern Spain and today it is often referred to as the California of Europe. This is a very fair description. Just as California was virtually undeveloped until the 1930s and then development took off, the Costa del Sol was a very sleepy backwater of Europe until the 1950s. Until then the entire area was extremely poor, but how beautiful it must have been – small fishing villages connected to each other simply by dirt tracks, sandy beaches with the fishing boats drawn up on the beach, remote hill villages (the *pueblos blancos*) – all backed by the majestic mountains of the Sierras. It is these very mountains that are partly to blame for the development which has already taken place and which is continuing. The entire coast is virtually frost free in the winter months. This makes the Costa del Sol a very pleasant place to live.

The sunny Costa del Sol

With 320 days of sunshine every year, and a climate that allows outdoor living virtually every day of the year, the residents of this coast enjoy a very good lifestyle. While the inhabitants of northern Europe are shivering and coping with everything winter can throw at them, the residents of the Costa del Sol are usually basking in sunshine under clear blue skies.

The building boom

This almost perfect climate is one of the main reasons behind the unprecedented building boom, aided by the fact that with modern communications it is increasingly easy for people to work and run companies in northern Europe but from a distance. Relocation therefore becomes a possibility.

During the 1960s the building boom was at the eastern end of the coast while the western end remained relatively unspoiled. This is changing rapidly and, within a few years, the entire coastline will be built-up. The area from Nerja to Gibraltar may eventually be very similar to greater Los Angeles.

The coast is changing but this brings prosperity to the region. It provides jobs for those who live here and necessitates the upgrading of the local infrastructure to cope with a larger population – new roads, more public transport, better shopping facilities, better communication facilities – in fact the infrastructure which is expected in the 21st century.

Choosing the part of the Costa del Sol which is right for you

With such a large stretch of coastline to choose from quite apart from the inland areas there will be a place which is right for you. No description of the area can replace the physical act of coming here and investigating for yourself, but the following descriptions might help you to narrow your initial search …

The eastern end – from Almunecar to Torrox

If we accept that the Costa begins at Almunecar, the coast between here and Nerja is probably the most beautiful stretch of coastline in the entire area. The coast road twists and turns above pretty, rock-lined coves as the Sierra de Tejeda sweeps down to the sea. Nerja itself is now very developed and is the first big resort in the Malaga section of the coast. This town was 'discovered' by the British in the early 1960s. Continuing to the west the next towns of any size are Torre del Mar and Torrox. Both are now being heavily developed due to their close proximity to Malaga airport but if you want to live in an area where there are large modern developments with an almost total expat community in the new developments, this could be the perfect area for you.

Malaga

Next stop on the coast is Malaga itself, one of Spain's major cities and the provincial capital. Malaga remains an essentially Spanish city and has been improved greatly in recent years with the construction of new man-made beaches all of which are maintained in superb condition. It is probably the one place on the coast where you will find real big-city culture with concerts, theatre (in Spanish of course) and museums. Picasso was born here and the city opened a new Picasso museum in 2003. Despite development, Malaga remains very Spanish.

Two coastal areas which are virtually suburbs of Malaga might also be worth considering, Rincon de la Victoria and Velez Malaga.

Torremolinos, Benalmadena and Fuengirola

Now we come to the Costa del Sol, that everyone knows from the holiday brochures: Torremolinos, Benalmadena and Fuengirola. These are true resort towns, which exist for the holidaymaker's pleasure. They are brash, noisy and busy, and the party can go on virtually all night. But if you want to live in an area that is very lively these places are hard to beat. The expat community is large – everything British that you could want is easily available. There are many British-run businesses and you may never have to so much as try to speak Spanish here. There is good public transport – buses and trains – so you may not even need a car. The expatriate infrastructure means that there are a huge number of British clubs, British restaurants and even British theatre.

From a purely personal point of view, I would not want to live there but I appreciate that for many potential residents the area is perfect. The other major benefit is that these towns are finished. They are already so built-up that there is very little room for new development so what you see is what you buy and will not change too dramatically in the future. The fact that they were developed almost 40 years ago also means that there is a lot of refurbishment going on in the area.

Calahonda to Marbella

Beyond Fuengirola the coast continues to be very highly developed but here there is still a lot of new development. There are cranes everywhere between Calahonda and Marbella and that wonderful view which your new property has this year may not exist in a year's time. I will deal with this very real fact of life on the coast later.

Calahonda is already very developed but its close neighbour, Puerto Cabopino is most pleasant, with a relatively low density of building.

Marbella – playground of the rich and famous – is next. Surprisingly, Marbella retains an absolutely charming old town of narrow streets with whitewashed houses and, in its centre, the stunningly beautiful Plaza de los Naranjos – Orange Square. This square, filled with orange trees laden with fruit becomes one large open-air restaurant in the warm summer evenings. In the rest of Marbella and its western suburb of Puerto Banus, money talks and talks loudly. Expensive cars, designer boutiques and private yachts the size of small ferries are much in evidence. Needless to say, property prices around the Marbella area are among the highest on the coast and still the building continues.

The western end

This was the part of the Costa del Sol that was originally much less developed. San Pedro de Alcantara remained quite Spanish for a long time when the town itself was more than one mile from the sea. Now, however, the area between the town and the beach has been developed beyond all recognition, and some of the worst traffic jams on the coast are in San Pedro. The older parts of the town remain very pleasant and there is also a very lively British expatriate community. Some areas are almost totally British with virtually all the shops and restaurants British-run and run for the British. These are the places where you can buy your English-style sausage rolls from a branch of a well-known frozen food outlet, your English books and cards, your English bed linen and then have a drink at an English bar. It really is little England in places!

San Pedro to Estepona

Coastal development continues between San Pedro and Estepona but this latter town has so far managed to remain very Spanish. The old town on the hill leading up to the church is delightful and should you decide to live here you would have Spanish neighbours, so an ability to speak the language would be a real benefit. The centre of Estepona has escaped the worst of the high-rise developments but there is now a lot of new building surrounding the town. In fact it is in this western end of the coast where the boom in building is currently taking place.

Why? Quite simply, the infrastructure – mentioned earlier – has improved. The coast road, which at one time was a nightmare bottleneck, has now been widened into a dual carriageway and a new toll motorway has been built a few miles inland so communication has improved. A few years ago nobody wanted to live here but now that is changing. The western end of the

Costa del Sol is now accessible and right along the coast almost to Gibraltar the landscape is full of cranes.

Towns such as Sabinillas, which only three years ago was a sleepy little Spanish town on the coast road with the main road running through it, is now being transformed by new apartment buildings and new supermarkets. Manilva town hall has plans for a new theme park, hotels where no hotels existed and 6,000 new homes to be built in the next two years.

This area also appeals to many British expatriates since it is close to Gibraltar which remains a little bit of the UK stuck on the tip of the Costa del Sol. Many Brits go there to shop. Many work there and live in Spain. Gibraltar also offers an alternative airport to Malaga (which is becoming increasingly busy with long delays during the height of the season). Currently there are far fewer flights and a much poorer choice of destinations from Gibraltar but things are improving. (Incidentally Gibraltar itself is very expensive to live in and is very crowded and noisy.)

On to Sotogrande

Continuing our journey along the western coast the next major resort is Sotogrande. This relatively new development is either a paradise for the potential settler or it may have no appeal whatsoever. Built around a new marina it offers an ambiance that is very international – almost American in style – wide palm-lined boulevards, modern apartment blocks and villas which would not look out of place in Beverly Hills. It is very much an international resort, which bears very little resemblance to real Spain. There are plans to turn this area into the polo capital of Europe. This fact alone will give the reader some idea of the style (and potential prices of property) of Sotogrande.

For those who would like to be close to Sotogrande but cannot afford Sotogrande prices you could look in Torreguidiaro, Guidiaro, San Enrique, Tesorillo or San Roque.

Alcaidesa

Beyond Sotogrande there is currently only one new resort before you reach Gibraltar – Alcaidesa. Still very new it has many apartments and townhouses many of which have spectacular views of Gibraltar and the North African coast. Alcaidesa will no doubt be an important resort area in the future since it is surrounded by some of the most prestigious golf courses on the Costa del Sol.

La Linea, Algeciras and Tarifa

We have almost reached the end of the western coastal area but there are three towns that deserve a mention. La Linea has never really been considered a potential destination for the British expatriate. It remains very, very Spanish but it is a big town with all the things needed for everyday life and it is very convenient for Gibraltar should you work there. Currently property prices in La Linea are very low compared to the rest of the coast but that is because the prices here are geared to the Spanish market and not to the expat. It could be a very interesting growth area for the future although it is not a pretty place.

Just before we reach our final coastal destination, I have to mention Algeciras, if only to say that I would be very surprised if anyone chose to relocate from the UK to there. It is one of Spain's major ports. It has some of the ugliest oil refineries imaginable and it really is a very big, industrial town and commercial seaport.

The final town on our coastal trip is Tarifa, where the Costa del Sol ends and the Costa de la Luz begins – in fact it is not really on the Costa del Sol although I have included it. Tarifa is Europe's most southerly town and is in fact only 12 miles from Africa. You almost feel as if you can touch the Rif Mountains in Morocco from here.

We are no longer on the Mediterranean – we have reached the Atlantic coast and now we begin to experience the Atlantic winds. Tarifa is the wind surfing capital of Spain and does offer some absolutely spectacular beaches. The old town retains its original walls and is absolutely delightful and truly Spanish. The newer areas are not quite so pleasant but I am sure that they will grow and expand in the future and Tarifa will become more important.

Leaving the coast behind

So far I have described the coastal area to which most new settlers have tended to move but increasingly people are considering the inland areas as the ideal relocation choice. These areas are populated with towns and villages that are still very much part of the real Spain and, generally, property prices are more reasonable at the moment but are rising rapidly.

The hill villages

If you remain south of the High Sierras, the weather remains delightful. Higher up in the hills it will be colder in the winter but it will also be cooler in the middle of summer and the mountains will protect you from northerly winds.

The choice of destinations here is very wide and should you be considering a more rural environment you really need to go exploring. The entire length of the coast from east to west is dotted with hill villages, white villages – the *pueblos blancos* – which have already been settled by the expatriate community. Competa, Frigiliana, Mijas and Benahavis have already lost much of their true Spanish atmosphere and the only Spanish you will hear spoken is probably by the cleaners or the gardeners. Some of these villages may only have a few hundred inhabitants.

Coin, Alhaurin, Cartama and Antequera

Larger towns such as Coin, Alhaurin, Cartama and Antequera, which are close to Malaga around the Guadalhorce River valley, are developing rapidly as target areas for expats but so far remain very Spanish. Living here, the ability to speak the language would be an advantage. There is development around these towns but not as much as on the coast itself and if you fancy a really rural lifestyle it is still possible to buy a finca or farmhouse at reasonable cost, although the prices are rising fast.

Some of these towns benefit from being in the Guadalhorce River valley or close to it because they have good public transport to Malaga itself by both bus and train. It is also a stunningly beautiful area with a very important agricultural focus. As a result it is unlikely to suffer from overdevelopment. The fruit harvest is still an important part of the local economy.

Further inland, areas such as Sedella are very beautiful and you are then approaching an area often referred to as the lake district.

Ojen and Istan

Two hill villages that must receive special mention are Ojen and Istan. They are both just inland of Marbella. They are both spectacularly beautiful and very Spanish but, because they do not have a Marbella postal address, the property prices are much more affordable even though they are just ten minutes from the glitz of Marbella.

There are many other beautiful white villages scattered through the Sierras. I cannot list them individually and I have to be honest and say that I have not visited all of them. The only way to decide in which one you would like to live is to visit as many as possible before making a final decision. But there are some factors which really need to be taken into consideration before you jump in and make offers on property.

Accessibility of your property

You need to seriously consider accessibility.

- If you are 20 miles from the coast at the end of a winding mountain road there may be no problems on a beautiful summer's day but what happens in winter when it rains?

- If the dream property which you find in the summer is at the end of a non surfaced track what happens when it rains and your car is not an off-road vehicle?

- If you buy a village house in a white village which clings precariously to the hillside can you cope with the fact that your car may have to be parked some distance from the front door?

- You may have to carry heavy shopping from your car.

- You may have elderly relatives who could not cope with steep slopes.

- You also need to think about the days when the sun does not shine – there are not many but they do exist.

- If you have a family you also need to think about the difficulties of the school run from a remote mountain village that may not be served by a school bus.

Summary

- Use this chapter to narrow down the areas you might consider as the perfect destination for your Spanish dream.

- Do you want to live where the expatriate community is already well developed and where you can live comfortably without learning Spanish?

- Do you want good access to public transport?

- Do you want to live in England with sun or do you want to live in real Spain?

- Are you prepared to learn Spanish?

Invest in a few good guide books and read about the areas which interest you – a few pounds spent now on guidebooks is a small investment to make to help you make the right decisions for the rest of your life.

If you have friends who have already made the move – talk to them and seek their advice. Then, take their advice and use it to help you make the right decisions.

3 The Climate

Climate is probably the first reason that makes anyone from northern Europe consider a move to the Costa del Sol but for some people it could also be a reason to make them regret their decision in the longer term. So what is the climate really like and how will you adjust to it when you actually live here?

A climate of extremes

The climate on the Costa del Sol could be considered to be one of extremes. There are long periods when there is no rain at all and the sun shines relentlessly onto a landscape that becomes more and more arid. June to the end of September is characterised by heat and dust. Then the rains arrive. The arid landscape suddenly bursts into bloom as the dormant seeds of the wild flowers spring back to life. October on the Costa del Sol is almost like spring in the UK.

The scorched grass on the hillsides turns green and there is life again. The very lack of rain, which creates this parched landscape, can also cause spectacular brush fires, which either start naturally or through the carelessness of man. Once more when the rains arrive this scorched earth springs back to life and within a very short period you would never know that there had been a fire at all.

Modern society has eased the problems of lack of rain and it is many years since there has actually been a drought on the Costa del Sol. Today, civilised communities can move water around countries and ensure that life will continue as we expect it to. We also have far more expertise in finding water reserves and drilling wells deep enough to provide water. This was not always the case and, after the Moorish occupation of this part of Spain ended, there were frequent periods when agriculture was difficult. The Moors had expertise in irrigation – their successors did not.

Is the summer too hot?

In one word – no!

It would be very wrong to say that the temperatures on the Costa del Sol are always perfect. We have just come through one of the hottest summers on record when temperatures rose to the low 40s Celsius day after day and there was no rain at all from the first week in May until the first week in October. In the sun it was very hot indeed but the moral is to stay out of the sun. In the shade the temperature was perfectly bearable and actually very pleasant. It is also amazing how your attitude changes when you live in a hot climate. Until moving to Spain we had enjoyed two or three holidays a year in the sun. The first thing we would do after arrival at our destination was to make straight for the beach or pool to bask in the sun.

No longer! When you are able to enjoy the sun virtually every day of the year it is no longer necessary to lie out in it just to prove you have been on holiday. Now we watch the holidaymakers turn red as they overdo their sunbathing. We stay in the shade.

Respecting the sun

The local population here has lived with the climate for centuries and they have learned to respect it. In order to survive summer you need to make sure that your house faces in the right direction. The Spanish themselves often buy east or north facing – if they buy south facing they do look at how they can avoid the heat of the summer sun. You must also respect climatic oddities. When the hot wind blows from the Sahara you need to close the windows to keep the wind out – not open them and hope you will have a cooling breeze.

The sun needs to be respected. It is powerful here and if you get too much of it you will feel even hotter because your skin is sunburnt.

One local factor, which can result in the heat of the summer being more bearable, is the fact that generally the relative humidity is low. Heat with high humidity is much more difficult to live with. We have found Florida or the Caribbean more difficult to cope with.

Summers are not too hot so long as you are sensible about the sun and the possible heat.

The winter months

There is a winter on the Costa del Sol but compared to what we experienced in the UK it is a delight. In fact the winter months can be the most beautiful of all and often winter days here are similar to summer days in the UK. The weather is characterised by warm sunny days and cool evenings when a log fire is necessary but it would be almost unheard of to actually light the fire during the daytime.

It is for this reason that many British retirees love to spend their winters on the Costa del Sol and return to the UK in summer to see friends and family. It is unusual for the temperature, even overnight, to drop much below 10 Celsius in the coastal area. Frost is unheard of and I do not think we will ever experience freezing fog or icy roads anywhere on the coast.

You do however need to be warned if you move further inland and on to higher ground. In the mountains there is snow and there can be a lot of it. There are ski resorts in the Sierra Nevada behind Malaga, and the Costa del Sol is one of the few places in the world where you can ski in the morning and lie on the beach in the afternoon.

The rain in Spain

If there is a negative about winter on the Costa del Sol it is rain – the rain in Spain does not just fall on the plain. It is possible to go for months without a single drop but when it arrives it is like a monsoon. It does not usually last for very long but it can be very dramatic. Roads are turned into rivers. Dried-up riverbeds, parched by the summer sun, can suddenly turn into raging torrents. Depending on the area in which you live it is possible to experience flash floods. This has caused a lot of damage to property in the past. Developers do not always respect a history of flash floods and in the course of building these wonderful new properties they have been known to inadvertently block dried-up river channels or even build on top of them. Only when the rain arrives do the residents realise the mistakes that have been made. Properties have been flooded, newly laid out gardens can disappear as the power of water takes over.

If you buy your dream property and it happens to be on the side of a steep hill you need to ensure that the existing storm drains are effective and that there has been no history of landslides locally. We have heard of relatively new properties sliding down the hillside. And not just properties: last year, part of the newly constructed coast road simply disappeared into the valley below following a period of very heavy rain. It was only six months old. Luckily there were no cars or lorries on that stretch at the time but the road still disappeared!

Dirt track or mud track?

The very heavy rain that we experience here can also be a

problem if you buy a dream property at the end of a dirt track. During the long, hot summer months you will have almost no problems apart from the amount of dust your car leaves behind when driving along the track. Come the rainy season that same dirt track could be impassable without a four-wheel drive vehicle and even then you could still have problems. There are also instances when dirt tracks have been surfaced using basic concrete – a sort of ridged concrete track. Again, it's no problem in the dry but, when it is raining heavily, some tyres can have problems getting a grip on the concrete, particularly if the track is on a hillside.

These are things you need to consider when the estate agent is showing you your potential dream on a beautiful sunny day. The estate agent will never tell you that access could be difficult when it rains and, until you experience it, you may never even consider that there could be a problem. You also need to accept that most property viewings are usually arranged at the time of year when the properties are presented at their best.

The climate is wonderful and is the reason why so many people from the north settle here but it needs to be respected. When Mother Nature throws her power at the Costa del Sol it can be dramatic.

Table 1 Average weather profile for the Costa del Sol (Malaga*)

	Spring	Summer	Autumn	Winter
Max temp (C)	21	29	23	17
Min temp (C)	13	21	16	8
Hours of sun	8	11	7	6
Monthly rain (mm)	46	0	64	61

* Inland temperatures and rainfall can be very different. Summer is much hotter and winter can be very cold and wet

Summary

- When selecting property consider the heat of the summer and the rain in the winter.

- Remember also if you view property in the mountains in the summer when the sun is shining there may be snow in the winter.

- Consider whether bad weather could affect access to your property.

4 Quality of Life

In the increasingly stressful world in which we live today, quality of life is one of the most important considerations in the decisions taken on where to live. Analysis of your current quality of life may make you want to rush into a change to try to make improvements. You must however make valued judgements.

What are the differences between life here and life back in the old country?

The quality of life compared to the UK

Although I have compared life here to life in the UK many of the comments could apply equally to other northern countries but since many of the comments come from personal experience, they may not apply if you live at present in a rural area. My experiences are derived from city life in the UK compared to suburban life on the Costa del Sol.

The fascinating fact here is that although we now live in Spain we still read British newspapers and watch British television, so we tend to see the old country which we know very well from a totally different perspective. Without being totally negative there do seem to be many problems today and the quality of life of the average Brit seems to be deteriorating.

The relative cost of living

The first consideration in any analysis of lifestyle has to be how much money is in your pocket. In the UK the Government, national and local, just seems to be taking more and more money out of the pockets of its citizens.

Just to live in the house in which we lived in SW London we would now be paying around £2,500 a year in Council Tax. In addition we would be paying heavily for water, not to mention gas and electricity bills to heat the house during the winter months. Contrast this with the Spanish equivalent of council tax on our apartment of around £190 per year and an urbanization charge of £1,200 per year but this charge includes maintenance of the communal gardens, the swimming pool and all our domestic water together with maintenance and insurance of common areas.

The overall tax burden on the average UK citizen just seems to rise all the time. Yes, there are taxes in Spain but they do appear to be much lower and more of your own money actually stays in your pocket. You do have to pay more yourself for the services that you decide you need or can afford.

Services in the UK are rising in price all the time. In our new life we pay considerably less for electricity, telephone and heating than we did in the UK.

Transport

UK public transport appears to be deteriorating all the time. The London Underground is plagued with problems. Mainline and commuter trains do not run on time and the long suffering public are being asked to pay more and more for a deteriorating service. Spanish railways are modern, efficient and tickets are inexpensive. In addition, new services are being planned all the time. The high-speed rail link between Madrid and Malaga is being constructed now. There are plans to extend the current rail system all the way from Fuengirola to Estepona to ease the amount of traffic along the coast road. When it is built it will be efficient and the fares will be cheap so people will use it. The bus system is efficient and offers modern, air-conditioned coaches, which run to a timetable that can be trusted. In most areas there is an efficient school bus system, which collects children from designated pick-up points along the route thus resulting in the school run being virtually non-existent. Mothers only need to take their children to the nearest bus stop.

Driving

Whenever new roads are planned in the UK, there has to be a public enquiry and many local people will oppose the building of them. Opposition to any new building seems to be a British disease. The UK is plagued with NIMBYs (Not In My Back Yard). On the Costa del Sol the authorities simply build the necessary roads when they are needed and where they are needed. The decisions are based on the needs of the community and not on the wishes of a few individuals. In one of our nearest towns a new road was built which divided the town and made it difficult for local people to get from one side of the town to the other. Almost immediately the road builders moved in again and put the new road into a tunnel. The building work only took six months and hardly inconvenienced the inhabitants at all. The result now is that through traffic goes into the tunnel and the town centre is quiet again.

When I now watch television coverage of the congestion on the motorways around major British cities, I wonder how I ever coped with it. The answer is, I knew nothing else. Traffic jams do occur here but never on the scale familiar to people back in the UK.

Car parking

In many British towns and cities, car parking is a nightmare and charges are very high. If you park in the wrong place you end up being clamped or towed away with an even higher charge to pay to retrieve your car. Yes, there are parking meters here. There are parking restrictions. However, once again, if the authorities believe there is a need for a new car park, they build it. We have never had problems parking in Spain and when we do use the car parks they are very cheap. The Spanish have realised that the car is here to stay so provision has to be made for it. There is also the pleasant fact that during siesta time – 2 till 5 in the afternoon – car parks are often free.

Keeping cars out of the city

The UK seems to be moving more and more towards various forms of congestion charging which to me seems to be totally anti-car in its aims and yet another way to take money out of the pocket of the motorist. In Spain the decision will be taken to build a bypass, even around very small towns, to take the cars away from the population and improve life for everyone.

Perhaps the reason why many services here are so much cheaper is that the companies providing the services are not being clobbered with more and more charges which, at the end of the day, have to be passed on to the customer in the form of higher costs.

Healthcare

Healthcare is another topic dealt with at greater length later in the book, but whenever we see TV or read newspaper articles about the state of the NHS in the UK we are appalled – and so pleased that we now live here. As everyone gets older, healthcare becomes more of an issue but I have to admit that I would hate to be really ill in the UK in the 21st century. Whatever money the Government throws at the NHS, it appears to make no difference. A total rethink is probably necessary but politically that would be very difficult to organise. The concept that the NHS should be free at the point of use just does not make sense – nothing is free. Someone, somewhere, somehow has to pay for it.

In Spain there are virtually no waiting lists for hospital admissions. Hospitals themselves are very modern and very well equipped. Hospital food is wonderful. Yes, in the public sector there are queues in the GP surgery just as there are in the UK but in the private GP sector there are no queues and your consultation can take as long as an hour. If you do not have health insurance this could cost you €40 – £28 at current exchange rates – but at least you know you are being treated as an individual and you are being listened to. In the UK if you phone up for an appointment with your GP you may be offered one a week later (perhaps even longer). In Spain you will often be offered an appointment later the same day. Compared to the situation in the UK this leads to a very positive attitude towards quality of life in the 21st century since we all need to see a doctor sometime.

The family

One major difference between lifestyle and quality of life here compared to that in the UK is the Spanish attitude towards family and family ties. The family as an entity has virtually disappeared in many urban areas in the old country. Spanish families still look after the family, whatever their ages. Children act the way British children did years ago and ultimately all the family look after their older relatives.

The Spanish state does not generally provide a lifeline for individuals who are not prepared to look after themselves. Yes, if people who cannot look after themselves find themselves in a retirement situation without any pension there is the possibility of a *Pensione non contributaria* but this is not the normal situation.

Social security

Like most modern democracies, Spain has a very good social security system but you receive nothing unless you have contributed. Unemployment benefit is only paid to people who have worked in the past – one year in six – and have found themselves unemployed. You have to work in Spain for 15 years before you can even start to contribute to a state pension scheme.

In terms of overall quality of life this is an important consideration since anyone who chooses to live here does need to be relatively self-sufficient. The state does not provide and, therefore, you will have to provide for yourself. But since the state is not paying out huge amounts looking after others, looking after yourself costs much less. Even if your total income is only your UK state pension, you should be able to live here comfortably if you can afford to buy a property. You will certainly live much better, with a better quality of life than that you would enjoy in the UK on a state pension.

The effects of climate

Climate and location also contribute to quality of life. I can still remember the horrors of the switch from UK summer time to UK winter time. Suddenly, you realised that for the next few months you would leave for work in the morning in the dark and return home again in the dark. The only time you saw your house in daylight was at the weekend. The clocks do change here as well but because you are closer to the equator there is a more even distribution of the hours of darkness and light.

Even in the middle of winter on the Costa del Sol there is daylight at around 8 am and the dark period of the day does not return until after 6 pm. So you will have almost three hours more daylight than you would enjoy even in the SE of England and if you happen to live in the north – considerably more. I was born in the West of Scotland and during the winter there it was dark until 10 am and it was dark again at 3.30 pm.

No more SAD

The other wonderful contribution to quality of life from this factor is that more often than not the hours of daylight are also hours of sunlight. The one thing that nobody should experience on the Costa del Sol is seasonal affective disorder – no more SAD. Quality of life really is improved by 320 days of sunshine every year. What we certainly do not miss from our old life in the UK is day after day of grey skies. I know I said earlier that Costa del Sol rain can be a very real problem but at least you know that it will probably only last for a short time and the sun will be back soon.

The negatives

Yes, there are negatives!

There is nowhere in the world where life could possibly be perfect all the time and if you are considering a permanent or semi-permanent move to the Costa it is only fair that you appreciate any potential negatives which might affect your life before you take the decision to relocate here. After all, the estate agents trying to sell you your dream property will not mention negatives even if they appreciate them – you might decide not to buy and they will not earn commission.

It could be too quiet in the winter

The Costa del Sol is primarily a holiday destination and is likely to remain so for the next few years. Despite the huge of amount of new development which is currently taking place there are a large number of properties which are empty for most of the year – these new properties are and may remain second homes or potential holiday rentals. This can be absolutely wonderful if you like your own company but if you are a gregarious person it could be a very real negative if you live here 52 weeks of the year and is something which I will return to when discussing your potential choice of the ideal property.

It could be too noisy in the summer

In the same vein because it is a potentially a holiday destination you can suddenly find that the wonderful quiet development in which you live and which you have come to appreciate suddenly becomes a madhouse in the height of the summer. There will be noise around the communal swimming pool. There will be screaming children – and believe me today's children while on holiday can really scream – and sometimes the parents appear to be totally oblivious to the noise they create.

Even if the urbanization in which you live has community rules about noise around the swimming pool late at night this does not mean that you will escape the noise. When people are on holiday and return from a restaurant or a bar in the early hours of the morning a dip in the pool can appear to be very appealing on a warm summer evening even if the community rules prohibit late night use of the pool. These same holidaymakers do not even consider the fact that there might actually be other individuals who live in the development and who may have to get up for work the next morning.

Also, since people live outdoors here for many months of the year, a group of people who do not respect others can be a bit of a distraction to the resident population if they sit on the terrace until the early hours of the morning drinking wine and chatting. It is an unfortunate fact of life that the greater the consumption of alcohol the louder the discussion.

Living in a big resort

The positive aspect of living in a big resort is that there will always be life there and even in the low season you will never feel isolated. The downside is that in the height of the holiday season the roads will be busier, the car parks will be busier and the restaurants will be full (although regular customers throughout the year can usually find a table!). It will take you much longer to do all the things you need to do to live your life normally and it might cause you some frustrations

Choice of the right location

In planning any move you also need to think very carefully about where you live now and how much you want your new environment to reflect the things that you have come to expect in life. If you have been accustomed to living in an urban environment or in a British village where services have always been available, the lack of these services in some parts of the coast could be a real negative. Even to buy the most basic items could mean getting in the car. This will not happen if you live in the heart of one of the big developed resorts but then you will have more noise at other times.

If you choose to live in the countryside and the access to your property is along a dirt track there may even be times when you cannot even get out to buy the basic necessities of life. You will therefore need to ensure that you always have everything you need just in case the rain arrives during the winter months.

Coping with the heat

The climate for us has always been a real positive but if you are truly the type of person who cannot cope with intense summer heat, the Costa del Sol could be a problem. You can escape if you find good shady areas but in July and August the temperatures in the sun can be cruel. We know many people who love living here for ten months of the year but they have to escape back to the UK in the height of the summer. If you think you might fall into this category it is better to consider this carefully before you select your ideal place to live.

Another aspect of the climate, which could be a negative for some people, is the fact that there are really no seasons on the Costa del Sol as you might have known them in England. Summers are hot, dry and dusty. Winters are cooler and wetter but many of the trees do not lose their leaves. In fact winter is more like an English summer with warm days and the occasional dull and wet day. You might actually miss spring or autumn. In fact, spring on the Costa del Sol really arrives in October when the first rain of winter arrives and everything starts to grow again. Over the winter period the countryside and gardens are full of flowers.

The expatriate community

A very strong positive for many people who relocate to the Costa del Sol is the size and strength of the expatriate community. Wherever you live you are likely to have many British friends. It is good to be able to enjoy this easy communication with others who now live in a foreign country in the language you have spoken all your life. This can lead to a real sense of security should you have problems. There will always be someone you can ring for help or advice.

The converse is that since the expat community is very close the community can become very incestuous. Everyone knows everyone else and that includes their personal business. Having lived in a big city in the UK there are times when we have found this unusual. If your personal background is in a small town you may find it absolutely ideal. If you like the anonymity of big city living you need to choose very carefully where you live. Depending on your own personality, you might actually resent the lack of privacy which life in an expatriate community can produce.

Entertainment and culture

Quality of life includes many things and among these could

be a love of cinema, theatre, the arts and museums. If this is an important factor in your current life you really do need to consider your choice of location here very carefully. It can take an hour to get to a cinema and even then the films may be shown in Spanish. There is very little theatre in English apart from one theatre in Fuengirola. There is opera and ballet but not on the same scale that you would expect in other areas of Europe and perhaps not even of the same standard.

Outside Malaga there are very few world-class museums. The Costa del Sol is very rich in history but can lack the culture that you may have come to love or indeed need in your life if you live close to a big city in the UK. Many people who live here return to the UK just to gorge themselves on theatre. Indeed, many of the local Spanish population do the same by going to Seville or Madrid.

There are beautiful towns to visit such as Ronda, the many hill villages and of course Malaga itself. There are wonderful excursions, like the train journey through the mountains from Algeciras to Ronda. You are within striking distance of Granada, a World Heritage Site; and slightly further away are Seville and Cordoba.

Travelling outside the Costa del Sol

You must also take into consideration that in moving to the Costa del Sol you will be closer to Africa than you are to Europe. Africa is 12 miles from Tarifa but to travel anywhere else in Europe takes hours. Travelling to Morocco is easy and fast.

Travelling outside the Costa del Sol can be a negative. If you are planning to move here and continue to run a business back in the UK, you will have no problems whatsoever. Availability of flights to most airports in the UK is good from Malaga and improving all the time from Gibraltar.

Table 2 Airline services serving the UK

From Malaga	From Gibraltar
(Most airports in the UK have a connection to Malaga)*	London (Gatwick or Luton) and Manchester
British Airways	British Airways
(GB Airways franchise)	(GB Airways franchise)
easyJet	Monarch
Flybe	
Iberia	
Monarch	
Various charters (which allow flight-only ticket purchases)	

* See appendix 4

However, if your business travel necessitates visits to other European or world cities you could have the most frustrating problems. Nearly every destination will involve travel via Madrid or Barcelona or even the need to fly back to the UK and then onwards from there to your final destination. Not only can this be very inconvenient if the flight times do not match up but it can also be very expensive. On one occasion I had to travel from the Costa del Sol to Vienna. This involved a day of travel each way and the fare was more expensive than that from London to New York. If you have to charge your travel costs to a client this could be a problem. In the case I have just described my air fare was actually more than the daily rate which I charged my client for the two days of work which I had been asked to do (so we had a teleconference!).

This is the chicken-and-egg syndrome. Malaga is not yet a major European business destination therefore connections to Europe and the rest of the world generally are not well catered for on scheduled flights. Most European destinations will require a routing through Madrid or Barcelona. If you plan to continue to work in a job that involves extensive travel from the Costa del Sol you really should look into the travel options very carefully before you make your final decision.

The frustrations you might encounter could seriously affect your overall impression of your new life in the longer term. Potential negatives must be considered before you make your final decision.

Summary

- Evaluate exactly what sort of lifestyle you want and need.

- Take into consideration the fact that the Costa del Sol is primarily a holiday destination at the moment.

- Think about life in an expatriate community and what that might entail.

- Think about the climate.

- Think about your travel needs and how important they are to your lifestyle.

- Consider your current and future income very carefully. The Spanish state does not provide and, if you do not have sufficient income, life could become very difficult.

- Work out in advance how much money you will need to live on – not just now, but in the future.

5 Property

How to choose the right property

When you take that very important decision to change your life and move to the Costa del Sol, perhaps permanently, the first important decision is where you want to live. Not only where do you want to live but in what type of property. What is your budget? What do you expect in your new life?

These questions are equally important whatever your age.

You need to choose location very carefully.

1   Does your chosen location offer the services you need for your new lifestyle? Is the property close to important facilities?

2   Is it close to good schools?

3   Will I need one car or two?

4   Will it be accessible at all times of the year with no problems?

These are only some of the questions and you must never let your heart rule your head when making any decision on property. You must remember that when you move to Spain you will not be on holiday. The first day in your new environment will be the first day of the rest of your life.

Location

In choosing property on the Costa del Sol the major factor is the choice of the right location. We all have dreams of that idyllic property in the sun with spectacular views. If the view is important and the reason why you like a property, be very, very careful. The view you enjoy today may not be the view you will have tomorrow. There is so much development taking place on the Costa del Sol and virtually every prime site near the coast is either being developed or could be in the future.

Only you can make the final decision but before making it you must consider carefully the possibility that new property could be built in front of you and destroy your view. Do not be lulled into a false sense of security because you are on high ground. Even steep hillsides are being blasted into platforms on which new apartments are now being built if that new platform has a view.

Most importantly, take any comments from your estate agent with a very large pinch of salt. Too often they will say that the land around your choice of property is too steep for building or they might claim that it is green space with no planning permission. If the property is surrounded by well tended agricultural land you might be safe but if the surroundings are being allowed to go wild it could be re-zoned for development. In addition take any comment about lack of planning permission with a very large pinch of salt.

Planning issues

Planning permission is not a problem for developers on the Costa del Sol! Buyers have been regularly caught in the past but when the new development starts it could be too late because after your property has been purchased reselling might prove to be more difficult with a new apartment block directly in front of your house. Remember always that the estate agent is there to sell you a property today rather than to help you fulfil the dreams you might have for tomorrow. We know of properties that had wonderful views or were in isolated but still accessible locations, which are now totally surrounded by new development. The value of these properties may have dropped by a large amount.

We have even overheard conversations where an 'estate agent' on the coast was discussing the potential deposit on 15 new apartments with a speculator and the developer had not even bought the land. If he had the deposits he could buy the land and then obtain planning permission! The developer could then use the argument that he had clients for his project as a lever to obtain planning permission. It is illegal to use deposits to fund building but it still happens and many have been caught out in the past.

Case histories

1 The established apartment

When we first moved here we moved into an established urban area that really was on the edge of the countryside. We were surrounded by open land and the local goatherd used to lead his flock of goats past our kitchen windows virtually every day. The land on the top of the hill next to us was officially green space with no planning permission for building. Three years later there are 250 apartments on the top of the hill (planning permission was only given after the building work started!). The goats have disappeared. A plot of land, which had planning permission for 4 villas, was developed to accommodate 16 townhouses.

It was a major change but not too difficult for us to live with since the development is behind us and our view to the front of our property has not really changed too much. However the sales brochure for the apartments contains an artist's impression which does not show the town houses which now effectively block the view from the lower floors of the apartment block and the sales literature for the town houses shows an empty hillside behind. The same developer is building both developments!

2 The Cortijo in the country

Good friends bought a country house for restoration. They bought it about eight years ago. The restored house is beautiful and has been featured in the Spanish equivalent of *House and Garden* and when we first knew it the location of the house was isolated, on the top of a hill with panoramic views on all sides. Access was initially via a dirt track on which they had concrete laid.

It really was paradise but over the last two years the land surrounding them has been taken over by developers and now there are new properties being built almost up to their front gates. Development also destroyed the access road, which they had paid for, and their metalled road has now reverted to a dirt track. Even a four-wheel drive vehicle does not guarantee access to the house when it rains – many of their visitors now have to make a detour of several kilometres just to reach the house from the opposite direction. We have also heard that the valley in front of this particular house will now be the site of a new golf course and 1200 apartments.

3 The off-plan purchase

Last year we watched a well-known relocation programme on British television in which prospective UK buyers were shown off-plan information on a new development of town houses close to where we live. We recognised the location immediately. The properties looked wonderful and the prices were within their budget. They made an offer for a house, which had not even been built, and appeared to be very happy.

Now that very same area is like a small town. The density of building is very high, much higher than they were told when they bought. There are future phases being built, which were not described to the buyers at the time, and there are other developers building on adjacent sites.

This is part of the problem of buying off-plan from an artist's impression but on the Costa del Sol so many properties are sold in this way at property exhibitions in the UK. Sometimes those who buy do not even bother with an inspection trip. Many who do buy off-plan are speculators who hope to make a healthy profit in the future when they resell.

If you are moving to the Costa del Sol to live here the one point I would make is that if you are spending your money on the property in which you and your family plan to live – choose very carefully and resist buying a picture.

I use these case histories to illustrate the fact that it is your money which is being spent and you really need to take as much advice as possible on your chosen location. You also need *your* Spanish lawyer to check out what plans might exist for future development although even when you do this you could still be caught out. When there are huge profits to be made from development there will always be ways for developers to get around the lack of planning permission. In some respects it is better to buy property in an area that has already reached a high level of development. At least you know that nothing else can be built there.

The infrastructure

In any newly developed area you also need to find out about water supplies – are they adequate at the moment, never mind in the future? Can the sewage system cope? Is electricity supply being overstretched? Are there enough telephone lines and are they in good condition? You must ask these questions and demand accurate answers. If you do not get a satisfactory answer, walk away from a potential deal no matter how much you like the property – there will be another property that is just as desirable. Estate agents are not going to volunteer the information that water supplies could be a problem.

If the area is already developed, return a day or two later to your dream location on your own without the agent and try to speak to people who already live there. Ask them for honest answers to your questions. If your chosen property is an apartment you need to check how well it is insulated for sound. In a new development close to us one new resident is very annoyed by the fact that not only does he hear the toilet flushing next door – he also hears what happens in the toilet.

Unfortunately on a short inspection trip this is not always possible. In addition, if you visit Spain with developers who organise inspection trips you may not even be given the opportunity to visit your chosen site alone. The agent will be alongside you every waking hour to try to clinch a sale.

Rural areas

The other possibility is to buy in a more rural area where there might be less incentive for developers to build property. Many buyers want sea views so this is where the developers congregate. Buying in rural areas however also brings potential problems. Your lawyer needs to check that all the building work is totally legal and that all taxes have been paid. Remember that taxes in Spain go with the property. Your lawyer also needs to check that there are no plans for new motorways or other construction work on your land or close to it because if the Local Authority decides to compulsory purchase your land, you might be offered very little in compensation.

> *We heard of English owners who had a finca with 10,000 square metres of land. This land is now under the new motorway. Having been promised compensation they moved out and when the compensation was offered the price was the equivalent of £5,000.*

Land grab

'Land grab' is a term often used to describe the compulsory purchase of land to build and/or improve public services and facilities. In 1994, the Valencian government passed a law to speed urban development. The purpose of the law was to ensure developments were built with sufficient public services and facilities. But bad drafting and subsequent abuse by unscrupulous developers resulted in some property owners having their land compulsorily purchased, at prices far below commercial values, and then receiving huge bills for the cost of improving the local roads and infrastructures.

The law enables property developers to ask that land be reclassified from rural to urban (thereby making development much easier) without the owners' permission. Publication of this change must be made, but only fifteen working days are allowed to make an objection. With many absentee holiday homeowners this notification is entirely inadequate.

This problem has been highlighted in the UK press and, ironically, has probably slowed development in the regions it has affected. Nothing like this has happened in Andalucia but it could!

Type of property

Urbanizations

Because of the nature of the property market on the Costa del Sol many properties you are likely to be shown (unless you move inland) will be in what is called an urbanization. Developers originally purchased the land and developed it for owner occupation but at the end of the day the entire area is an independent legal community in which the residents pay for the upkeep of the roads and the common services. These are not covered by the payments you make to the town hall.

You therefore need to ask your estate agent whether or not the property of your dreams is an independent property or part of an urbanization and if it is, what are the annual charges? Some of the charges can be very high especially in up-market urbanizations in places like Marbella. If you do not pay these charges, under

Spanish law you run the risk of losing your property. It may be repossessed by the community to pay any outstanding costs and ignorance of the fact that you had to pay in the first place is no defence.

In urbanizations there are basically three types of property: apartments, townhouses and villas. Everyone appreciates that apartments are part of a community because you have people above, below and to each side. Townhouses are not so immediately recognised as being a community property since back in the UK many townhouses are totally freehold with each owner being self-sufficient. A villa in the UK would probably never be considered to be part of a community since it would be freehold and you would be responsible for everything.

Not so on the Costa del Sol – you might find that you are severely restricted in what you would like to do in terms of development of your villa because it is a property in which the community has an interest. We know people who have bought what they considered to be a freehold, detached villa only to find later that they have to pay high community charges and they cannot make large-scale changes to their own property without the prior agreement of their neighbours.

Individual villas

These are probably everyone's dream property but they are also the most expensive. They have often been individually designed and built. Large gardens are common as are swimming pools. In most cases they have been designed to take full advantage of the views but even with this type of property that view could be obscured by new building. If this happens, it could wipe thousands of Euros off the value of your investment.

Country property

On the other hand if you move to a country area you could end up with much more freedom to be the master of your own destiny but if you buy in the country you need to ask your lawyer to check that your dream property is totally legal.

- Did it have planning permission in the first place?

- Is the size of the house you are buying now in accordance with the *escritura* – the title deeds?

- If not, has the current owner paid any fines which might still exist for increasing the size of the house without official permission?

I will return to this later but you must remember that in Spain, bills (or fines) accompany the property so if the previous owner does a runner without paying what is due, *you* will be liable and *you* will have to pay.

There is a culture here of extending, developing or improving property without asking for planning permission on the basis that if discovered you will probably pay less in fines than you might have done for the planning permission in the first place. This is fine if you plan to stay in the house for a long time since many of the potential penalties disappear after a few years. Your transgression may never be discovered but when you sell – or more importantly when you buy – could be the time that the previous owners are found out.

There has also unfortunately been a tradition in the past for owners of a plot of land to build a house on it with no planning permission whatsoever. As far as the title deeds are concerned, the land exists but the house does not. The authorities are beginning to tighten up on this.

Country properties can make very fine houses but there is often much work to be done to bring them up to the standard to which you might be accustomed. Many older properties may not have electricity, town water or adequate sewage disposal. They may be miles from the nearest telephone connections but this can be overcome using mobile or satellite telephones.

Plus valia

You also need to ask your lawyer to check that a tax called the *Plus valia* was paid by the seller. This is a tax based on the increased value of the land as a result of development since the last time the land or property was sold and is usually paid by the seller. However, if the seller does not pay, the tax will stay with the property until it is paid. Some friends bought a villa that had been lived in for many years by an elderly couple who on moving did not pay this tax. Some time later the local authority simply took the *Plus valia* from our friends' bank account because they had signed a direct debit at the town hall to allow the local authority to collect local taxes direct from their bank account.

A traditional town house

Buying a traditional townhouse in a village or a town can move you right into the centre of the true Spanish experience. You will have a higher proportion of Spanish neighbours and you will undoubtedly pick up the language. Even if you buy an unrestored house, access to modern facilities should be easy. The only real negative is that life in the centre of a Spanish town or village can be noisy and, unlike town houses in the UK, you will be very lucky to find a house with any garden. Your only outside space may be an internal courtyard or a roof terrace. The flat roofs of many of these town houses are used by the local population to dry the laundry.

Buying a ruin or a potential demolition to rebuild

Another new law which has recently been introduced in Andalucia might prove to be a problem for some buyers in the longer term. In the past, if you bought a property in the country on which there was an existing house or a ruin it was not difficult to demolish the existing property and rebuild that dream property which you had always wanted.

New laws will ban this. If the ruin does not have a roof you cannot rebuild it. If the existing property is only 60 square metres – that is all you can build if you demolish and build something new. This is a way for the authorities to preserve the countryside as it is now. It could also be a problem for buyers who planned to build on the land which they purchased a few years ago with a view to building in the future when funds permitted.

Keeping warm in the winter

Whatever your age you should also consider the options for heating the property in the winter months. You may see the property in the height of the summer and never even stop to consider that from November until March you will need heating in the evenings.

- By far the most economical source of heating is a log-burning open fire or stove. Logs are plentiful and very inexpensive – especially if you buy them or have them delivered from the wood yard. (NB It is not advisable to store firewood in the house – risk of termites.)

- Electric radiators are a bit more expensive to run but very efficient.

- There is no town gas on the Costa del Sol so you will need to use bottled gas. If you choose this form of heating, gas burning convector heaters are not too expensive to run. However, steer well clear of gas-fired central heating. We know people who have this only to find that it is possible to use an entire bottle of gas in a day to provide heat.

Heating costs money in the winter months but if you buy property with large south facing windows you may need to consider installing air-conditioning for the summer months. This too costs money to run and for it to be efficient you would need to keep the windows closed in the summer which to me slightly defeats the object of moving to a sunnier climate in the first place.

Property to suit your lifestyle

The young family

If you are younger with a young family you need to choose property which is close to good local schools. You need to think about the fact that your children will want to visit their friends and you will be the chauffeur. If the property you choose is isolated, will you be able to find a babysitter should you want to have an evening out on your own? Will you need two cars or will you be able to live with only one?

The retiree

If you are older and planning to retire to the Costa del Sol there are other considerations. The beautiful three-floor town house may be no problem now but what happens when you get older and the stairs become a problem? Are you close to good local doctors? If you are in a more remote area how well is it covered by the emergency services, should you become ill? Is there a good local community which will provide you with leisure facilities? Are you choosing a property which is in an area which is mainly organised for holidays? If so, you have to realise that in the winter months it could be very quiet indeed whereas in the summer months it could be very noisy. Many people choose a location which faces the community swimming pool because it looks wonderful – a dream come true – but they may be viewing the property outside the main holiday season. Everyone has dreamt of looking out over a beautiful blue swimming pool. That same swimming pool in July and August could become an absolute nightmare when it is thronged with families on holiday with screaming children.

Golf property

Others choose property which is front line to a golf course. Wonderful if you play golf but if the fairways are directly in front of your terrace you will be plagued by the constant procession of golfers past your terrace in the golfing season which in Spain is most of the year.

Beach front

To many, a front line to the beach seems bliss. Yes it is – in the summer – but the Mediterranean is not always the placid blue sea of the holiday brochures. Storms do occur and beaches can be eroded by winter storms so if your dream property is first line to the beach you need to check how secure it is against the elements. In addition beach front properties could be affected by the damage that salt-laden air can do to the fabric of your home or your possessions. Check beach-front properties very carefully for damp.

Renting property

If you are making your first move to the Costa del Sol and you are undecided about the exact area in which you want to settle it makes a lot of sense to rent first and use that initial location as a base from which to look around to find the property you finally want to buy. After all, if you rent a property which you do not like you can move out very easily and try somewhere else.

Renting is not difficult and there are many properties available for medium- to long-term rentals. In the majority of cases they will be furnished and rents can be surprisingly low. Just casting a quick look through one of the local English language newspapers at the time of writing shows that there are many properties of all sizes available for less than €1,000 per month. So, if you rent for your first three months on the Costa del Sol it could cost you almost £2,000 but it could save you considerably more than this should you make the wrong decision by buying too quickly. Holiday rentals can be very expensive in the high season but in the low season you should be able to negotiate very good deals with property owners here. After all, if you do not rent the property it might actually be empty so the owners are prepared to do a deal.

Buying property

Immediately you decide that your future really does lie on the Costa del Sol, you should buy. Prices are increasing rapidly at the moment and the bubble shows very little sign of bursting in the foreseeable future especially with the enlargement of the European Union. That wonderful property which you can afford this year may be unaffordable by next year. Buying is not difficult, it is just a bit different from the process in the UK. Detailed information on buying is included in many other books and it would not be appropriate for me to repeat what fellow authors have already written but in principle you need to add 10% to the official price of any property which you are shown, in order to cover the costs of buying. A good local Spanish lawyer will take you through the process in detail. The purpose of this book is to tell you what it is like to live on the Costa del Sol.

Legal implications

The legal aspects of buying property properly belong to the buying process but there are some which could have implications on your life here either before or after you have moved and some which may come back to haunt you if you make the wrong decisions at the time of buying.

Official and unofficial prices

When buying property in Spain it is quite common (although illegal) to have two property prices. One price is the actual buying price exclusive of all fees and taxes – this is the price you actually pay – in a combination of personal cheque or mortgage plus cash. The other price is the price on the *escritura* and this can be considerably lower. Everyone involved in the buying process is aware of what is going on but generally they turn a blind eye to it. It is done because taxes paid on the transaction are paid on the official price, not the full price, so it is a way of avoiding tax for both buyer and seller although it is the seller who saves more tax. On one occasion we were shown a property which we absolutely loved but the seller only wanted to put 30% of the price on the *escritura*. We walked away with no hesitation.

Personally I do not think that any buyer should turn a blind eye to this process. If you need a mortgage the mortgage may only be granted as a proportion of the official price, the *escritura* price. If you are paying cash, in theory you do not need to worry. After all you will pay the same price in the end but if you are counting on a mortgage of say 60% of the buying price and the official buying price is 20% less than the real price then your maximum mortgage could be a maximum of 48% of the actual price which is being asked. This could make a tremendous difference to the affordability of your chosen property.

As I said, this book is not meant to be a comprehensive guide to the buying process, but agreeing to a low official price for your selected property could have serious implications for your future life in Spain. By this time the seller who benefited from a low official price will be long gone. What could happen to you?

The local town hall can check up on the reported price you paid for your property and if they believe that you have underpaid they can question the difference between what you paid and their valuation of the property. You could also be fined for this underpayment. It does not happen very often but it can happen. Incidentally, this could also happen if you are offered a 'bargain' property – a property which someone may need to sell very quickly because they are desperate for the money. I know of people who have been challenged by the local town hall on the actual price they paid and they have had real problems in proving that this was actually the price because the difference in prices is usually paid in cash and there may be no receipts. Spanish law does not encourage the sale of property under market price.

The other problem you are storing up for yourself in your new life is the fact that should you wish to sell your Spanish property you will be liable for capital gains tax and this will be based on the difference between the official buying price and the official selling price of the property when you sell. In simple terms if you initially agree to a low official price when you first buy you will in future have to find a buyer who also agrees to a low selling price. Fine at the moment, but if the authorities decide to tighten up on the rules what you think now is a major saving could become a millstone around your neck in a few years.

The black economy

The so-called 'black' economy is very prevalent in Spain. Cash is used as a means of avoiding tax and some experts have reckoned that this hidden part of the economy is worth more than 20% of the Spanish gross domestic product. Many of these same experts are calling for the government to tighten up on this aspect of Spanish life. If this happens, agreeing now to a low official purchase price could be storing up future problems for you and your family.

Mortgages

If you are retiring to the Costa del Sol you may have enough equity in your property in the UK to allow you to sell up and buy your new property in Spain without a mortgage. This is the ideal situation – no debts.

However there will be many readers of this book who do need to raise a mortgage in order to fund the purchase of their property in Spain. As I explained earlier you may only be able to raise a mortgage on the official price of a property so, when viewing and, to avoid disappointment, you do need to check the official asking price before you make any offer. Before you are resident in Spain you may be limited to a mortgage of 60–70% of this official purchase price depending on your lender. Assuming prices are in order you then need to decide where you propose to raise the money.

The Spanish bank

The first option should be your Spanish bank. They will lend to individuals even before they have *residencia,* and your mortgage will be at the Eurozone rate of interest which is lower than that of a UK mortgage and is likely to remain so in the future. Your repayments will be in Euros and should the Euro rise in value against the pound you could end up paying much more, but I think this is a risk worth taking. In addition, if you are working in Spain, your income will be in Euros so you will have no worries over exchange rates. Currently there is great competition between the various banks to provide mortgages.

The UK bank

The next option should be your UK bank. Many UK banks are very happy to lend to customers with a good credit record who wish to buy property overseas. The first negative in this scenario is that your mortgage will be in sterling so if the pound loses value against the Euro the amount you will have to repay will rise. Secondly the interest rate will be at the Sterling rate which is currently higher than the Euro rate and is likely to remain so in the foreseeable future. However, on the positive side, your repayments will be in Sterling from your UK bank account so you will not be paying commission on the transfer of money into Euros.

The mortgage broker

The final option is to arrange a mortgage through the many companies who operate on the Costa del Sol or on the Internet who claim they will arrange mortgages for UK residents who want to buy in Spain. The services they offer are in the main totally honest and legal but they will charge you for arranging your mortgage. You are not being ripped off but you could probably arrange a mortgage at no charge if you go through the normal channels. Why arrange a mortgage through an intermediary who has to make money somehow, when you could go direct to the lender, possibly even the same lender which the mortgage broker will use? Many of these companies exist to arrange mortgages for individuals who would have difficulties in arranging mortgages through other channels.

The first point of contact must be the Spanish bank with whom you have opened a local account.

The buying process simplified

1 Find your property.

2 Make an offer – your estate agent should be able to guide you on what offer might be accepted.

3 Appoint a Spanish lawyer (*abogado*) if you do not yet have one – it is not in your best interests to use

the vendor's lawyer or one used by the developers if you are buying new property.

4   Apply for your mortgage.

5   The estate agent will then obtain a copy of the *nota simple* (simple note) from the Land Registry which will prove that the vendor is actually entitled to sell the property and there are no debts outstanding.

6   A purchase contract will then be drawn up which is signed by both parties.

7   You are then required to pay a deposit (usually 10% which is non-refundable).

8   Your lawyer will then obtain a copy of the owner's *escritura* (title deeds) plus a certificate from the Town Hall which states the names of the residents of the property (*the empadronamiento*). If you are buying furnished, an inventory of the furnishings and fittings should also be obtained by your lawyer. He will also check that all utility bills, local rates and (if appropriate) community charges have been paid.

9   When all documentation is considered satisfactory and your mortgage has been approved, vendor, buyer, lawyer and sometimes a few other people arrange a meeting at the local *Notario*, Notary (a Government official) who will check all the documentation. He will also make sure that you understand what you are signing and the *Escritura de compraventa* will then be duly signed by both

parties. (If you cannot attend this meeting you can appoint a legal representative on your behalf.)

10 The property is now yours!

The *Escritura de compraventa* will then be sent to the property registration office and in due course you will receive your *Registro de la propriedad*.

You should allow 10% of the property value declared on the *escritura* to cover the costs of buying. This sum will cover the following taxes and fees:

- Transfer tax and VAT (*IVA*)   7%

- Stamp duty on new build property   0.5%

- *Plus valia* (the vendor may pay this)   0.5%

- Fee for the *Notario*   0.5%

- Property Register fee   0.5%

- Lawyer's fee   1%

Summary

- The wrong decisions on the property you buy initially could seriously affect your quality of life in the future.

- If in any doubt, rent first.

- Choose according to what you need – not what you want.

- Decide what you want to buy and not what your estate agent thinks you should buy.

- Be careful on the legal aspects and take good legal advice.

- Consider your surroundings very carefully – what could be built around you which could seriously affect your quality of life.

- Trust your own instincts and make decisions accordingly.

- Do not be afraid to ask searching questions – after all, it is *your* money which is being spent.

- Do not store up long-term problems on location, legal aspects, finance and so on. You are the one who will live with these problems.

- Above all do not make long-term decisions based on information which you have not checked out at first hand.

- Take care over the black money issue – it is not always in your best interests to accept a low price on the *escritura*.

- Should you require a mortgage be very careful and ask the right questions before you commit yourself to any mortgage deal.

- When searching for a mortgage start with the Spanish banks, then British banks and if you draw a blank with them, then consider a mortgage broker as a source of funding.

6 Banks and Money

Banking in Spain is now very good and is comparable to any other western European country but it can cause frustrations in your day-to-day life. The process can still be very bureaucratic and slow and a trip to the bank can take quite a long time since the queues move very slowly. Queues in the local bank can now be avoided by the use of on-line banking which is becoming more developed in Spain. When banking on-line you will find that most banks will have an English language service.

Which bank?

Any trip down the high street of a typical medium-sized town will indicate that there are many different banks. Some are very small and basically serve the local area. Others are regional, such as the Banco de Andalucia on the Costa del Sol, whilst others are Spanish branches of major multinational banking groups. The ultimate choice of bank is entirely down to you and your own needs but it is probably better to avoid the smallest banks since their range of services might be more limited. The first rule of thumb is to select a bank which is convenient to where you live.

Opening a bank account

It is now very easy to open a bank account as an EU citizen and your estate agent or your lawyer here will be very happy to introduce you to the local bank manager. A personal introduction is by far the easiest way to open an account. When you go to the bank you will need your passport, evidence that you own property in Spain and your NIE number (see later). You will be surprised on the Costa del Sol that a visit to most Spanish banks will result in a meeting with someone who speaks fluent English. This takes many of the worries away from the transactions you need to complete. Until you are resident your bank account will be designated as a foreigner's account.

Within a short time you will have your bank account number, a cheque book and a debit card which you can use for shopping or cash withdrawals from a cash dispenser (ATM machine). The card is the most valuable since cheque books are virtually useless in Spain. Cheques are not trusted and are very rarely used or even accepted, even by another bank. We used only six cheques in three years from our chequebook. Spain remains a society where most payments are made by cash or by a debit card with suitable proof of identity. In the past this would have been your passport but until you have *residencia* in Spain and the corresponding identity card, a very useful proof of identity is a UK photo-driving licence. I would strongly recommend that any UK citizen planning to live here changes their driving licence immediately. It is an invaluable aid to proving your identity.

Direct debits

The other valuable service which you must use to pay all your regular bills is the direct debit. This takes the worry out of paying on time. It also avoids the possibility that if you do not pay on time you will be fined. Virtually all national and local tax liability will result in a fine if you do not pay by the appointed date and as a result tax collection is possibly less of a worry if you have arranged to pay all taxes by direct debit or standing order.

Bank statements

Unlike the UK where you receive one statement a month on your current account while on deposit accounts you might only receive one statement per quarter, Spanish banks seem to issue a statement every time a bill is paid and in addition they send you a monthly statement. There is a plus side to this since you know exactly where you are in terms of payments made but unfortunately it costs money to issue so many pieces of paper and it is you, the customer, who pays for this. Bank charges can appear to be quite high even when you are not using the account on a regular basis.

The other problem with your regular statements is the fact that from many banks they will be in Spanish – and why not, you now live in Spain. Initially we had to go through virtually every statement armed with a dictionary just to check what payments had actually been made. You can ask at your local bank whether or not it is possible to have a statement in English. If it is, it can be very convenient. On the other hand if you bank with the local branch of any well known UK-based bank you will almost certainly receive a statement in English on request.

Interestingly the debit card issued to a UK national by a Spanish bank will probably result in the instructions on the screen of the ATM machine appearing in English. This is a wonderful service.

Returning to the question of bank charges we did make an interesting discovery recently and it is one worth following up with your local bank. We had been accustomed to charges for direct debits, withdrawals of cash from the ATM machine and other services and we never questioned these charges. For personal reasons we deposited a sizeable sum in our current account in Spain and suddenly we received a message on the ATM machine that the withdrawal was commission free. You should ask your local bank what balance you need to maintain in order to qualify for this service since it will vary from bank to bank.

Credit cards

All the credit cards you have in the UK before your move here will be accepted, such is the nature of international banking today. The only warning I would give to you is that if you want to maintain your UK credit cards you should set up a direct debit for the minimum monthly payment with the issuing company in order to save yourself long term problems.

Increasingly companies are moving their call centres and their billing offices offshore to countries like India or the Philippines. This is fine for them and probably saves on overheads but such is the nature of the postal system between the point of origin of your monthly statement and its receipt in Spain that it can take three weeks to reach you and even if you pay on the day of receipt, it can take three weeks for your payment to reach the company. You will already be two weeks late in payment and if this happens repeatedly you might suddenly find that the company withdraws your card through no real fault of yours and this could result in you being listed as a bad credit risk which could cause problems in the future. I am currently in discussion with a major charge card company which has done just that after a history of 23 years during which I held their card.

It is also possible for you to have a Spanish-issued credit card should that be more convenient.

Coping with exchange rate fluctuations

Spain is now part of the Eurozone. When the Euro was first introduced it dropped quite dramatically in value but it has recovered recently. Currency fluctuations can be a nightmare on two counts. If you are at the stage of buying your dream property and your capital is in Sterling, a move of a few cents in the value of the Euro compared to the pound can make a major difference to the final price. If your ongoing income is in Sterling an increase in the value of the Euro could have a dramatic effect on your buying power. Equally if your move to Spain depends on a mortgage which is either in Euros or has to be paid in pounds converted to Euros you could find your outgoings changing dramatically.

Until the UK becomes a member of the Eurozone there is no real or permanent way in which you can get round these problems but there are things you can do to minimise them as much as possible. You will probably find that the majority of expatriate Brits would love to see the UK enter the Eurozone.

One way is to pre-buy your Euros if you are going through the process of buying property. Even this is a bit of a gamble because Sterling could rise against the Euro the day after you have bought your currency but this option does at least allow you to budget for an exact figure on the transaction which you know cannot change.

Long-term finances

When working out your long-term finances you really need to consider the possibility that the pound could drop against the Euro and if this happens could you have problems in the longer term? You may have a retirement income in Sterling, you may intend to run a business from Spain billing your UK client companies in Sterling. If so, you need to consider whether or not your income or your business could sustain a 20% drop in revenue due simply to the exchange rate. Since we moved to Spain the value of the pound against the Euro has dropped by 12.5%. Our income is therefore 12.5% lower than it was in terms of purchasing power here.

Another potential action which helps is to transfer as much money as possible from the UK as infrequently as possible. When you transfer a large amount the exchange rate you will be offered will be far closer to the commercial rate. The commercial rate is always higher than the tourist rate by quite a few cents to the pound. If you are transferring several thousand pounds this can make a huge difference.

Remember also that if you are a UK pensioner you can arrange for your state pension to be paid directly into your Spanish bank account in Euros and you should not be charged commission on the transfer.

Investment opportunities

If you plan to retire to the Costa del Sol, have sold up totally in the UK and therefore have capital to invest to provide an income for the rest of your life or if you are younger and plan to be successful and then, by investing the proceeds of your income be very, very careful where you invest this money.

The fly-by-night operator

On the Costa del Sol you could be unfortunate enough to find yourself in contact with what is often referred to as the fly-by-night operator. These financial advisors advertise in the press and on other media such as the Internet or they may even canvass you by telephone. Many of their advertisements are in the form of advertorials in the English language press. It looks like an article about finance but it is actually a paid-for-page of advertising.

The carrot is a very good apparent rate of return for your money compared to other current investment opportunities. You are the bait. You obviously want a good investment to make a healthy profit and they are just waiting to take your money. We have read of people who have lost virtually all of their life savings through entrusting their capital to such companies.

They will often appear to be very reputable businesses with very luxurious offices. They appear to be very respectable. They are very good salesmen and on occasions it can even appear to be difficult to organise an appointment with them because they appear to be so busy helping people to make a fortune. The salesmen will be very good at talking to you and they may even blind you with financial jargon which you do not really understand. They will try to convince you that the investments they propose will outperform anything else currently on the market and they will of course try to minimise any risk which might be involved.

When pressed they will admit that risk is always there but your potential return will be so good it is worth taking the gamble. These very nice people are there to help you get rich!

These companies will often try to persuade you to make quick decisions because, after all, if you hesitate you may never have the same opportunity again. The offer may not be available next week! If you make a quick decision it may mean (and probably does mean) that you have not had the time to contact another financial advisor who might advise you that what they are offering may not actually be such a good investment after all.

They will provide you with testimonials from other satisfied customers who appear to have made money from their investments. Sometimes their clients do make money short term and allow themselves to be used for testimonials but it is your long-term future you have to consider. In fact there are cases recorded where the investments have been set up in such a way as to show an initial dramatic return on the investment. It is only a few months later that this starts to change.

Identifying the fly-by-night operator

The first step you, as a potential investor, must take into account is to identify the company which could be a fly-by-night operator. You can check with the Directorate of Investors – the CNMV – who have an English-language Website on www.cnmv.es. This will at least be able to tell you if the company in question is recognised and authorised by the Spanish authorities and the Bank of Spain. Many people have contacted the CNMV only after they have lost their money and by then it is too late to do anything.

You need to ask questions as to whether the investment on offer is the right one for you. You need time to consider any proposals and perhaps even have them explained to you in front of your lawyer or other financial expert known to you personally.

You should also check how long the company to whom you are considering entrusting your money has actually been in business, the qualifications of the directors and their experience in the financial markets into which your money is going to disappear, what commission they propose to charge you and, most importantly, how do you get your money back should you decide to pull out of the investment.

This is too good to be true!

Deals which appear to be too good to be true are often just that – they are too good to be true. If the stock market is returning an investment of let's say 5% why should another investment return 10% if it does not involve a considerable gamble. Such investments may indeed return a much higher percentage but they are really only suited to very young investors who can afford to take the risk – even if they lose everything, they can start all over again. They are not suitable for the investment of one's life savings.

One problem which has faced investors who have lost considerable sums of money through high risk investment programmes in the past is the problem of legal retribution. The company to whom you plan to entrust your life savings may not be recognised or even registered in Spain and if you are a Brit, being ripped off by your fellow Brit, the Spanish legal system may not put your problem at the front of the queue should you decide to take legal action.

The other factor which has been a nightmare to some British investors is that they put their life savings into Gibraltar registered companies. They thought this was safe because Gibraltar is 'British', but the financial regulators in the UK do not always recognise these companies.

At the end of the day it is your money and you should attend all meetings prepared to take careful notes of the meeting and with a determination not to hand over any money until you are absolutely certain where it will be invested. Do not sign anything until you have taken good independent financial advice.

Summary

- Open a bank account with the nearest convenient bank.

- Arrange to pay all your Spanish bills by direct debit.

- Until you have *residencia* get yourself a UK photo-driving licence as proof of identity.

- Check what balance level you need to maintain to benefit from commission-free banking.

- Work out your long-term finances based on possible devaluation of the pound against the Euro

- Set up direct debits to pay your UK credit card bills.

- Transfer larger amounts of money from your UK accounts as infrequently as possible.

- Be very careful about investing money with companies who promise an above-average rate of return.

- Always take independent financial advice from individuals who do not stand to profit from your investment activities.

7 The Cost of Living

Spain is no longer the very cheap country that it once was. The cost of living has risen over the last ten years but it is still considerably cheaper than many of the countries of northern Europe. It is almost impossible to be totally objective in this section since your cost of living will depend on what you want to buy and how you propose to live. As a result, the cost of living here could be very, very low indeed or it might be very similar to your present costs. All I can do is to generalise and leave you, the reader, to draw your own conclusions. Appendix 2, showing typical supermarket prices, might give you some impression of prices on the Costa del Sol relative to those in the UK.

Your style of life

I have called this section your style of life rather than your lifestyle. If you relocate to Spain and you want to live in exactly the same way as you did in the UK you might actually find that there is very little difference between costs here and what you might have spent in the UK. If you want to buy British food all the time, life will be expensive. When shopping in Spanish supermarkets the difference in cost between the Spanish brand or the UK brand of a similar product can be very dramatic indeed. Some brands of British sauces or pickle can be two or three times what you would pay in the UK. The same rule applies to things like butter or cheese. Choose Spanish butter, or find Spanish cheeses that are similar to those with which you are familiar, and they will cost very little compared to the prices charged for English brands of butter or cheddar cheese. Choose to live in 'the UK with sun' and the cost of living could be quite high.

Meat and fish

If your idea of heaven is a typical roast beef Sunday lunch you will find that beef is relatively expensive since there is virtually no tradition of beef farming on the Costa del Sol, whereas pork and chicken are relatively cheap. Beef on the Costa del Sol is probably no cheaper than it is in the UK.

If you love fish, you will be in paradise. The Mediterranean is full of the most wonderful seafood, and the wet fish counter in the local supermarket is an incredible sight. The prices of fish such as monkfish are about a quarter of what they would be in the UK. Prawns and other shellfish are so cheap that the prices will amaze you. The overall choice is fantastic.

Fruit and vegetables

Vegetables and fruit are very cheap so long as you buy what is grown locally when it is in season. Don't buy imported produce unless you must have it and accept that it is a luxury. Buy the locally grown product and you will find that even luxury vegetables like asparagus are cheaper than you could ever imagine. Strawberries in season are bought by the crateful, and oranges are so cheap that it would be criminal not to buy a juicer and make your own freshly prepared orange juice. Why anyone should purchase cartons of orange juice on the Costa del Sol is a complete mystery to me when you can buy five kilos of fresh oranges for the equivalent of £2.00! It's even more of a crime to buy the synthetic 'orange' drinks (whose brand names I cannot mention) just because the kids are used to them in the UK. Hot tip: the place to buy your oranges or other citrus fruits is at the roadside, direct from the person who has grown them.

Avocados are almost given away when they are in season – they almost fall off the trees – and they grow so profusely that you almost need to find a cookery book which tells you 101 recipes for the use of an avocado.

Wine and spirits

Local Spanish wine is inexpensive. At the time of writing it is possible to buy perfectly drinkable, everyday wine for less than

£1.00 per bottle. So long as you buy Spanish wine, even very well known brands are considerably cheaper than you would expect to pay back in the UK. However if you are a wine snob you will find that the prices of imported wines can be very similar to the prices you would have expected to pay before you moved here.

Similarly, the price of the harder stuff can be high if you do not buy sensibly. If you like a gin and tonic and the only gin you will consider is the well-known brand sold in a green bottle in the UK you could find it to be relatively expensive compared to the local Spanish equivalent. I would challenge anyone to tell the difference after it has been mixed with the tonic water!

A Spanish or British lifestyle?

We never cease to be amazed by the number of UK expatriates who move to the Costa del Sol and still want to live in the same way as they lived before they moved. They visit English shops to buy English food and even buy frozen food imported from the UK. They travel down the coast to shop in Gibraltar in a well-known English supermarket, and all the time they pay way over the odds in order to continue eating those brands of food they have been buying for years. Interestingly, we have friends who live in Gibraltar who now choose to shop in Spain because the food prices are much lower and the quality is probably better.

Make the change to living in Spain, living in the Spanish style and you will find that your food costs can drop dramatically. Your cost of living will be considerably lower than you ever expected and the quality of food will be dramatically better.

The only concession we have made to our former life in the UK is to buy meat from an English style butcher because we can still buy English cuts of meat. Every country chops up carcasses in a different way so it can be a benefit to buy the cuts with which you are familiar. This is no different from some former colleagues of mine who were French, and who bought their meat from the French butcher in South Kensington in London because he sold the French cuts with which they were familiar. Apart from this one concession, we buy everything else in the same way as the locals. We buy Spanish brands. We shop in Spanish supermarkets, and we buy local produce when it is in season and which has probably been grown organically without any premium being added to the price for this 'privilege'. As a result our weekly shopping bill is probably about 30% lower than it was in London and we live very well (if not better since we eat far more fresh produce).

The cost of running your home

The cost of running your home is affected dramatically by the climate. The warmer winters mean that you will spend less on heating – there is almost no reason to have central heating operating for most of the day. Heating is only really necessary in the evening, especially between November and April. The type of energy you use can also affect your cost of living. When we lived in the UK we had gas central heating, and electricity for cooking and lighting. In Spain we currently use electricity for cooking and top-up heating when necessary (as we did in London) but we use a log burner as our main source of heating. What are the relative costs?

Electricity

Electricity bills in Spain appear to be much lower than they ever were in the UK despite the fact that many people in Spain think electricity is expensive. For us, a typical monthly cost during the winter months for cooking, lighting and supplementary heating is around 25% less than the bills we were accustomed to in the UK for a similar use of electricity.

Gas

Outside some of the major cities in Spain there is no town gas. Should you have gas-fired appliances you will need to buy bottled gas – but it is very cheap. When you buy a property that has gas appliances you will almost certainly inherit the gas bottles. These can be replaced for less than €10 at the nearest depot. We found in our first apartment here – where we cooked by gas and had gas-fired hot water supplies – that one bottle lasted for approximately six weeks. I think this is very good value for money and certainly much cheaper than gas supplies in the UK. There is a little bit more inconvenience since you need to ensure that there is always a replacement bottle available but this is not really a problem.

We also know many people who use gas bottles to operate radiators and, once more, the cost is not excessive. However, using bottled gas to run a full central heating system can be expensive. A gas-fired central heating system can use one bottle of gas per day. Avoid gas-fired central heating!

Living fires

If you live on the Costa del Sol during the winter months the most efficient and also the most pleasant form of heating is a living fire, which burns logs. You may buy a property with an open fireplace in which logs can be burnt. This is fine but it is possible to have very efficient log burners installed which cost very little and because they are enclosed they are potentially much safer and many also have the benefit of fan assistance to blow hot air throughout your property – they are log burning fan heaters.

The supply of logs seems to be inexhaustible. You have various choices. You can either go to the log yard and fill the car up with logs or there are many small companies who will deliver logs to your home. This year we have chosen the second route because it is much easier and we currently have deliveries of logs which last us for up to six weeks for less than £50.00. Compared to the cost of gas central heating or electricity in the UK, I think this is very good value for money and a real fire looks so wonderful. After all we will only have to pay for logs for three to four months of the year.

One word of warning however: logs are also available from many garages, but bought from this source they can prove to be expensive and are often not as good as those bought in the log yard since they have not been cut and dried in the sun during the previous summer. These logs are what would be referred to as 'green' wood. The logs from the specialist suppliers tend to be hard wood, which has been properly dried, and as a result it burns superbly and produces a lot of heat.

Household repairs

This is the one area where you do need to be very careful. There are many UK expatriates who make a very good living here by charging their fellow countrymen the prices which they would have expected to pay in the UK for household repairs or redecoration – and they then ask for the money to be paid in cash and they do not supply a VAT receipt. Whenever you need to call in someone to redecorate, sort out your plumbing or your electrical problems you should call in the expat contractors and then check their estimate with a local contractor. You might be surprised by the difference in cost between the two.

Only you can make the decision as to whom you give the work, but we have known occasions when people have paid £1,000 (in cash) just to have their living room and a hallway redecorated. This is not a typical Spanish price and is a classic example of an expat ripping off a new arrival on the Costa del Sol.

So long as there is a constant supply of new arrivals prepared to pay such exorbitant prices the practice will continue. If you need work done on your property, whatever the work, I would suggest that you arrange for local builders to do the work for you. You should also insist on receiving a VAT receipt.

Remember also that it may be false economy to have household repairs or renovation work done for cash. When you eventually decide to sell your property you will almost certainly be liable for capital gains tax but the only costs you can offset against your tax liabilities are those costs for which you can provide receipts showing that local VAT has been paid. Without these receipts you cannot claim.

Telephones

The Spanish national telephone service, *Telefonica*, is a modern, state-of-the-art service and it costs no more than the equivalent service in the UK. In many ways it actually provides a better service. We were surprised to find an automatic telephone answering service included with our bills. Our experience has always been very positive in moving into apartments which already had the line connected when we have asked for the line charges to be transferred to our name.

We have, however, heard of people moving into new property who had to wait for several weeks to have a new line connected. This does not happen very often in new urbanizations but people moving to new property in the country without a telephone line have often had to wait several weeks or even months to have a telephone connected. We have also found *Telefonica* very good when it comes to dealing with problems. They can always find an English-speaking customer care operator – would you find a Spanish-speaking operator in the UK?

Mobile phones

Mobile services are also very good and we were surprised that we were able to buy a new chip for our existing mobile with no problems whatsoever in Spain. We did not have to throw away the old handset whereas in the UK one is generally led to believe that if you want to change your supplier, be it on account or pay-as-you-go the first thing you need do is buy a new telephone. The fact that you do not need to buy a new handset can be a very real advantage if you do not plan to spend 12 months of the year on the Costa del Sol. You can buy a chip to use here and if you go back to the UK you can remove this from your phone and reinsert the UK chip. One handset can therefore be used in both countries.

Local dialling codes

- Malaga Province 952

- Cadiz Province 956

The Internet

Internet access is another matter. Initially I had a connection through a very good provider that offered local call charging for Internet access. The service was good but it did crash on occasions and I thought that the annual charge seemed a bit high, so I changed to another provider. I now find that while their service appears to be better, I am paying more for my telephone calls when I do go on-line. When I challenged the new provider on this they tried to persuade me to switch to an ADSL line – this may mean nothing to some readers but to others they will see the sense of this. If you use e-mail and the Internet a lot this would be the sensible option and it is very easy to organise in Spain and it is not expensive (as little as €10 per month).

Insurance services

Insurance is the one thing we all need nowadays, whether it be for the fabric of your house, its contents, your car or even for your health. In Spain, insurance costs much less than it does in the UK, unless you have moved from a very rural part of the UK.

Home insurance

If you decide to buy a property in an urbanization, the chances are that the insurance of the buildings is included in the annual urbanization charge. You need to check this with your estate agent at the time of purchase. If not, you are likely to find that the cost of insuring the buildings is much less than the equivalent cost in the UK basically because the cost of rebuilding, should there be a claim, is much lower.

What about contents? I cannot generalise on this, since contents insurance obviously depends on where you live, the relative risk of crime that might result in a claim to the insurance company, and also on what you own and the value you put on it. We have found, however, that the cost of contents insurance in our properties in Spain is considerably cheaper than that in SW London. In fact, insurance for approximately the same value is about one third of the cost we had to pay before we came here. I have not quoted actual prices, since costs depend on the company selected and the cover requested. From our experience, insurance of your worldly possessions will be much cheaper here.

Car insurance

Car insurance is certainly much cheaper than it is in SE of England on a Spanish-registered car. Currently we drive the sports derivative of a well-known super-mini and our insurance, fully comprehensive, is approximately one third of the equivalent cost in the old country and that includes roadside assistance. Take that cost off and the insurance would be about one quarter of the cost. OK, I have to admit that we are both over 50 and that reduces our insurance payments, and we do have maximum no claims discount but many people considering a move to Spain will be in the same situation. Whatever your situation you are likely to find that car insurance on a Spanish-registered car will be considerably lower here.

Health insurance

Health insurance is discussed at length in Chapter 10 Healthcare, but the bottom line is that it is much cheaper here. When I left the UK some three years ago a well-known insurance company offered to continue the private healthcare policy that I had enjoyed (as a perk) as an employee of the company that I had just left. The premium quoted was £170 every month. I do not know what that policy would cost now, but I do know that I have private health insurance in Spain for just over one quarter of that cost per month. This private health insurance covers hospital care, GP care, and an annual visit to a dental hygienist. This is much better value for money and actually provides me with healthcare that is infinitely better than anything I could expect in the UK.

Shopping

Earlier I described the relative costs for everyday food shopping but what about the other items you might need to buy on the Costa del Sol?

Clothes

Shopping for clothes is a mixed bag. The first point is that the climate means that you immediately save on the need to have a totally different winter and summer wardrobe. For most of the year what would be regarded as summer clothes in the UK can be worn here. Women are certainly less likely to feel the need to buy a new winter coat on a regular basis and for men there is far less need to wear tailored suits or formal shirts even for business. This is an immediate saving.

During the summer months everyone tends to live in shorts and T-shirts and these can be bought very cheaply in the local markets if all you want (or need) is the basics. In fact we know many people here who go to the local market in the spring and buy a supply of T-shirts for that year at very good prices and at the end of the summer season they just throw them away and start all over again the following year.

If you happen to be a label freak – which I once was – then you will find that designer clothes in Spain can be expensive, possibly more so than in the UK, since you need to go to the large department stores to find them and, with less competition, prices can be high.

Shoes

The undoubted bargain in Spain is shoes. They are beautifully made and you can choose to buy them on the market, in the supermarkets or in the department stores. Wherever you buy the quality will be excellent for the price paid and the choice will be very wide indeed. The other major bargain in the shoe stakes is sandals. So many people wear them through the spring, summer and autumn with the result that there is a huge and very competitive market, which results in the prices being one third to one half of the prices in the UK. Never bring sandals with you from England to the Costa del Sol.

Household goods

Household linen, towels and similar items are considerably cheaper. When we first moved here we had an apartment which we rented out for holidays and we decided that the one thing renters would appreciate would be good bed linen and towels. It actually cost very little to supply this and the quality was good. Another positive is that when buying ready-made curtains they are normally sold singly – you then buy the number of individual curtains that are necessary for the size of your window.

Electrical goods are likely to be much cheaper than they are in the UK and it is probably not worth the cost of transporting them to Spain. Certainly, when it comes to items like washing machines, your UK model may not work here. Most properties are set up for cold fill only for washing machines so many UK machines, which need a hot and cold fill, will not operate in Spain. Other white goods are very well priced and there is a lot of competition between the various stores, which helps to keep the prices low. British televisions will work if your signal source is UK-based satellite, but you may have problems if you want to watch Spanish television on a standard aerial. Televisions in Spain are very competitively priced and, once more, there is a very wide choice.

Smaller electrical items are probably priced on a par with the UK now. Similarly CDs, DVDs and videos are really no different in price here than they are back in England and if you want a very wide choice of entertainment software you are probably better advised to buy it on the Internet if you have access. The choice is greater and the prices are lower even if you have to pay for postage and packing and deliveries are usually within a few days.

Furniture

Furniture in this part of Spain may appear to be potentially more expensive than in the UK, mainly due to the fact that there are not so many shops selling flat-packed furniture. However the furniture stores on the Costa del Sol are actually very stylish and if you accept that you are buying good design and very well made items then the prices do not seem to be so high.

Cars

Cars in Spain were much cheaper at one time, but the differences have been eroded as the prices in the UK have dropped. Now there is really very little difference in the prices of most mainstream models. The one thing that is less well developed in Spain is the second-hand car market. The main dealers obviously have second-hand vehicles for sale but there are far fewer second-hand car dealers since the transfer of vehicles from one person to another is more complicated because of the tax situation. The local population tend to drive their cars into the ground, and then they replace them or use them as a down payment for finance on a new car.

Car servicing is considerably cheaper than we were accustomed to when we lived in the SE of England, even in the main dealerships. Overall, the cost of running a car here is much lower since apart from buying, servicing and repairs, fuel is about one third cheaper than it is in the UK.

Shopping when you do not actually want to buy!

I have to be honest and say that this is one area where you could be disappointed depending on what you want from your shopping experience. When we lived in SW London we enjoyed going to the nearest high street to spend a couple of hours just browsing on a Saturday afternoon. There was nothing that we particularly wanted or indeed needed to buy but we could window shop. We could browse in one of the big chain record shops or in the local bookshops. We could window shop the antique shops and all the other little independent suppliers. Sometimes we did buy. Other times we did not but it was a pleasant experience.

In the coastal area of the Costa del Sol this is much more difficult to do. There are big shopping malls where many of the high street names familiar to the Brits have outlets and there are lots of fast food restaurants. You could be in the UK and if you like shopping malls it will be heaven. All the shops are open from 10 in the morning until 10 in the evening.

If you go to the town centres of many of the towns however you will not find the shopping experience you would have in the UK. In addition there is the other complication that in the town centres many shops close for siesta so if you want to spend a leisurely afternoon shopping or window shopping, everything is closed. This can be very frustrating.

Markets

The various markets that exist along the coast are a very real part of life. Depending on where you live there will be a market close by virtually every day of the week. If you visit several in succession you will soon realise that it is the same market traders who move from one town to another during the course of a week but they can be a wonderful place to shop for the essentials of life.

The merchandise on offer ranges from fruit and vegetables of the most incredible quality grown locally, to the entire range of household necessities like towels and bed linen, all very competitively priced. You will also find shoe sellers and a wide range of clothing (much of it pirated designer-label clothes). Due to the closeness of the Costa del Sol to Africa there will also be many stalls selling goods of North African origin – ornaments, pottery, rugs and even wall fountains. The prices are competitive, but if you really want to buy products made in Morocco it would probably be cheaper to make the day trip to Tangier and buy direct. These markets are also the only places in mainland Europe where I have seen fake watches and pirated CDs and DVDs sold so openly.

Strangely, many of these markets do not sell meat, fish or cheese.

What income do you need?

This question is almost impossible to answer because everyone lives in a different way and has different priorities in life. If your lifestyle demands that you eat fillet steak and drink French wine on a regular basis, eat out virtually all the time and have a wild social life it could be could be quite – or even very – expensive to live on the Costa del Sol. If, however, you like to live more simply, life could be remarkably inexpensive.

The first important factor income-wise, is your debt liability. If you have no mortgage, no credit card debts and no hire purchase agreements you will be surprised how little you need to live comfortably. We know people here who live on a basic UK state pension and live well, even if their lives are not luxurious. Those with a basic pension plus a top-up occupational pension live very well indeed. For a couple with no children to worry about, no debts and no mortgage, I would estimate that if you have £10,000 a year income you could live well so long as you are not extravagant. With £15,000 you will live very well and, above that figure, you will have a very comfortable lifestyle especially if you are over retirement age and qualify for state healthcare. After all, the official, absolute basic wage in Spain is not much more than £300 per month and this is considered to be enough to live on! Check out Appendix 1, which lists our annual expenditure. We enjoy a very comfortable lifestyle.

The cost of living for a family

For a younger family, things will be different. If you work in Spain and pay Spanish social security you will qualify for state healthcare, but if your circumstances are different you may need top-up private healthcare. Similarly, if you are happy for your children to go to state schools in Spain you will not have to pay for private education, which although cheaper than the UK is still a cost. A family will also need to have a bigger car and possibly a bigger house and all this will affect overall financial needs but, ultimately, I would have to say that the cost of living is considerably lower than it is in most parts of the UK. On this basis if your earning potential is equal to that you would have in the UK you will live much more comfortably.

Plan ahead

Before taking the plunge, and moving your family to Spain you must sit down and work out how you propose to live here, what lifestyle you would like to have and, based on the information in this book and other sources of information, work out what income you might need to live on. Add a bit more for unforeseen expenses and then decide whether or not you can afford to make the move. Do this before you move and you will have no unpleasant surprises. Move on a whim, without working out your personal finances, and the results could be catastrophic for your family.

It is a big enough change to move country – if you then end up with financial worries on top of the move your life could be difficult. So many have moved in the past without making these calculations and have lived to regret it. We know people who have used up virtually all their life savings because they did not do their homework. You also need to work out how you will finance any debts you might have. If the debts are in sterling and the pound loses value against the Euro, your debt will be higher. Can you cope with this?

Appendix 1 includes a chart that shows our expenditure as two adults, with a separate column into which you can put your estimate of your own family needs. I have also included representative supermarket food costs averaged between the SE of the UK and from Devon and have compared these to the cost of similar items in Spain.

Summary

- The cost of living is lower than in the UK.

- Live like the Spanish and your cost of living will be very reasonable.

- Live as if you are in the UK with sun and there may be very little difference.

- Food can be very cheap.

- You will need to buy fewer new clothes.

- Household goods are basically much cheaper.

- Insurance and other household expenditure is less expensive.

- Work out your finances before you take the plunge to move.

8 Living Legally

As an EU citizen it is, to some extent, up to you how legal you want to be when you live in Spain since the EU has legislated for the free movement of its citizens. Despite this, individual states still have their own legal framework. Some of the points I make in this chapter may not be the way in which many people may choose to live here and, in real terms, if they do not meet the regulations in force they may actually be living as illegal immigrants, even if they are EU residents, but for the moment they get away with it. This may not always be the case.

The *Gestor*

One of the first things you should do when you first move to Spain (or even before you make the final move) is to find yourself a *gestor,* a fiscal advisor. He or she will act as an intermediary between you and all the complications of Spanish officialdom. A good *gestor* will take care of all the paperwork necessary for the purpose of paying local taxes, local income tax, car tax, *residencia,* for registering for healthcare and virtually all the other bureaucratic problems you might face. The good thing is that the charges for this service are very reasonable when you consider the load that is taken off your shoulders.

The NIE number

The *Numero de Identificacion de Extranjeros,* (identification number for foreigners), is one of the first bureaucratic necessities which you must attend to when you come to live in Spain. You should go to your local police station with your passport, a copy of your passport, two passport photographs, proof of residence in Spain and complete the relevant forms.

Your local lawyer, your estate agent, your *gestor* or a local friend who already lives here can help you organise this. The first step is probably to ask the estate agent to help you organise an NIE number. Most will be very happy to do this as part of the service they have provided in finding you a property and after all they have already earned commission from the vendor. What you do not need to do is to pay any company to organise an NIE number on your behalf. Paying for this service is not necessary – the NIE number is available free and you should not have to pay to obtain it.

Companies who charge a large fee are basically operating a scam – it is so easy to organise by yourself. If you are afraid of filling in the forms because they are in Spanish, your *gestor* will do it and I am informed that this should currently cost you around €40.

There are many people living here who have not bothered to organise an NIE number but without it, it is difficult to buy a car, organise insurance or carry out many other financial dealings. If you choose to follow no other legal rules, I would strongly suggest that you get an NIE number. I also suspect that there are many people who live on the Costa del Sol who do not even know that they should have applied for an NIE number because no one told them they should.

Registration at the town hall

Officially you should do this but, once more, I know many foreign residents in Spain have not registered. When you first arrive you should go to the town hall with a copy of the *escritura* – the *copia simple* – for your property and complete the form which registers you on the census of the local population. This is another example of Spanish bureaucracy but it potentially has some very positive benefits. Local authority services including police, post office, availability of school places and many others are based on the official census figures. If people do not register the services may not be as good as you might want but the town hall will say in its defence that they are catering for the number of people who officially live in the local community.

In addition, under new EU legislation, EU citizens registered on this census can not only vote in local elections but they can also stand for election. If this happened more often it could have a dramatic effect on local politics since in many areas of the Costa del Sol the non-Spanish population might actually outnumber the locals. Voting power could have major effects on your potential life in Spain in the longer term. There is also the fact that foreign residents here could put themselves forward as potential local councillors. They would probably have to be able to speak Spanish but if there were more councillors from the expatriate community, representing the interests of that community, local government might work in a very different way.

Paying your local taxes

Even if you chose to ignore the other rules and regulations, you must attend to this. The local tax, IBI (*Impuesto de bienes immuebles)* is effectively the Spanish equivalent of Council Tax in the UK. It is based on the assessed value of your property and if you do not pay it the failure to pay will catch up with you some day. When you come to sell the property you will have to pay and non-payment in the past can result in some quite hefty fines being levied. The good thing is that compared to similar taxes in the UK the IBI is very reasonable indeed, so there really is no excuse not to pay it.

Go to the town hall. Sign the appropriate documents and a direct debit form for the IBI and then just forget about it. At least in this respect your house will be legal. You will not be liable for fines and when you come to sell at some stage in the future and you will have no problems.

Residencia

This is the difficult one. According to Spanish law if you plan to spend more than six months in any one year in Spain or you do spend more than six months in any one year in Spain, you should apply for *residencia* (residency). I have to say that we have many friends who have lived in Spain for many years who have never applied, whatever their personal reasons, and many have no intention of ever applying for *residencia*.

It is not difficult to obtain. You need to visit the local *commisario* with:

- your passport,

- a copy of your NIE number,

- three passport photographs,

- evidence that you have private health insurance or that you qualify for state healthcare because of age or the fact that you are employed in Spain,

- a letter from your Spanish bank showing your annual income and your current bank balance, and

- evidence of your annual income.

You do need to be able to demonstrate that your income is above the Spanish minimum, which will obviously change from year to year.

When you go to this meeting you will be fingerprinted and, in about six months time, a *residencia* card will be issued. This card has to be renewed every five years but from the day it is issued it is your identification in Spain. You can then go back to your bank and register your bank accounts from non-resident to resident status. Your *residencia* card is the equivalent of a passport and should be carried with you at all times. The only time in the future when you will need a passport is when you leave Spain on holiday.

There are benefits to having *residencia*. The most important is that if you only have one property in Spain and you wish to sell it you will not be liable for capital gains tax so long as you buy another property in Spain within three years.

Once you have *residencia* you will be liable for Spanish income tax, which will have to be paid in Spain rather than in the UK. This may be one reason why so many people have not taken out *residencia*. If you prefer to be taxed in the UK, *residencia* could be a problem.

One of the problems which faces people nowadays is the decision on where they should be officially registered if they are EU citizens. Even if you spend more than six months a year in Spain you may still have an official address in the UK so neither the UK authorities nor the Spanish authorities know in which country you spend most of your time. It would be difficult for either country to find out since passports are not swiped at each entry or exit from or into the countries. Essentially you are moving from one country to another with no barriers to movement but neither country knows where you actually live and this is legal at the moment. If you no longer have an address in the UK you should apply for *residencia*.

Tax issues

It is an unfortunate fact of modern life that we all have to pay taxes and there is no government that makes this a simple procedure. There are several taxes that you may have to pay in Spain even before you have *residencia*, and the only simple way to organise your tax situation is through your *gestor*. He can advise you on your personal tax situation and possibly even suggest ways in which you can minimise your taxes and remain within the law.

The positive is that taxes in Spain are generally low – certainly lower than the UK in most circumstances. As part of the EU, Spain has treaties with other European countries that should ensure that you only pay tax in one country, although there are exceptions. The first major exception is that a UK government pension can only be taxed in the UK. The other major exception is that inheritance tax *(impuesto sobre sucesiones y donaciones)* on Spanish-owned assets is only payable in Spain and cannot be directed back to the UK where you pay no inheritance tax whatsoever until you have assets of around £260,000. Inheritance tax in Spain kicks in at a much lower level. So what taxes will you have to pay?

Property tax

If you are officially non-resident in Spain you are liable for wealth tax and unearned income tax on your Spanish property *(patrimonio & renta)*. The wealth tax is currently levied at 0.2% of the property value on the *escritura,* the rateable value of the property (*valor catastral*) or the market value while the unearned income tax (*renta*) is based on the assumption by the Spanish authorities that if you have a property in Spain and you are not officially resident, you must be renting it out). Currently this tax is 25% of 1.1% of the rateable value. Now you know why you need a *gestor*! The tax situation is complex and it is better to pay someone else to sort it out for you

If you have *residencia* and you only own one property you do not pay all these taxes but you do have to pay them on second properties. You will still be liable for the wealth tax. If you only own one property perhaps it would be a benefit to have the status of being a resident.

Income tax

Resident

If you are resident in Spain, income tax is payable on both earned and unearned income from worldwide sources. There are a number of allowances which can be offset against your tax liability related to age, dependants, pension contributions and mortgages but in real terms the only person who can really help you through this maze of regulations is the *gestor*. Your income tax liability is likely to be considerably lower in Spain than it might be if you still lived in the UK but I am not a tax expert and would not presume to give advice in this book. Entire books have been written on this topic. Take professional advice!

Non-resident

If you are non-resident or still waiting for *residencia* to be granted the situation is different and much easier to explain. Any declared income in Spain is taxed at a flat rate of 25% and you cannot offset allowances against your tax liability.

Capital gains tax

Whatever your legal status in Spain, resident or non-resident, you could find yourself with a liability for capital gains tax. This will happen if you sell Spanish assets and for most expatriates this asset will be their home. With non-resident status there is a flat rate of 35% payable on the difference between the official buying price and the official selling price. If you should decide to sell and you have non-resident status, 5% of the selling price will automatically be taken from the sale by the buyer's lawyer and paid to the local town hall against your CGT liability. There is no way you can avoid this.

One way of reducing your CGT liability is to ensure that you have the correct receipts, showing that VAT has been paid on any improvements made to your property. This unfortunately does not happen very often since so many expatriates use the services of expatriate tradesmen who are working for cash and do not issue receipts. Fine at the time of having the work done but it could pose problems for you in the future. You can also offset the costs of buying and selling against your CGT liability.

If you are resident, any CGT liable on the sale of your property will be collected through your Spanish income tax and you will be allowed a fixed deduction or an allowance for inflation before the tax is collected. For residents over 65 any capital gain is tax-free.

For non-residents the tax is fixed at a flat rate of 35% but if you have owned the property for more than two years there is an allowance for inflation but the age exemption does not apply. There are however many examples of non-residents who have paid the 5% withholding tax and moved their money out of Spain without paying another penny of CGT – that is why the

5% tax on the total value of the property was introduced in the first place.

Wealth tax (patrimonio)

I have already discussed this in the property tax section and if you have *residencia* you are liable for this tax on your worldwide assets: property, vehicles, jewellery, investments and cash in the bank, less any liabilities such as mortgages. With resident status each individual has a tax-free allowance, which is currently €110,000 per person. There is no allowance if you are non-resident. Once more your *gestor* can help you with this tax. The tax is payable on a sliding scale according to the level of your 'wealth'.

Inheritance tax

This is the real tax minefield in Spain and you should contact your *gestor* to discuss your potential liability and ways in which you might minimise it. The problem with inheritance tax is that it is very difficult to legitimately avoid since if a property is held in joint names any sale requires the signature of both parties and if one is deceased there is no way that both can sign.

Inheritance tax is payable on any property or assets including money in the bank and cars owned in Spain or indeed any other assets. It is the one tax that is not the subject of agreements between EU states and there also is no exemption between husband and wife even if the property is in joint names – each member of the partnership holds an equal share in Spanish law and therefore must pay the tax on the share of the deceased. This could cause problems but once more, consult your *gestor*. Unmarried couples on the Costa del Sol can now register their relationship at the local town hall and in return they will qualify for the same rights as a married couple so long as their partnership is registered.

There are different levels of inheritance tax payable depending on the relationship between the donor and the recipient.

One legitimate way of avoiding inheritance tax is to register your Spanish property as a company under Spanish law. If you do this at the time of buying it is very simple. If you do it at a later stage you will have to 'sell' your property to the company and this will incur selling charges and the appropriate taxes. The other potential negative is that the company will be liable for taxes every year so unless your property is a very expensive one it may not be a good solution. Once more – take advice!

Wills

If you have property in Spain you should have a Spanish will even if you already have a will in the UK. An EU citizen who lives in Spain can usually dispose of property according to the law of his/her state of origin but should you die in Spain without a Spanish will your assets could be dealt with immediately under Spanish law or there could be a delay while your UK will goes to probate back in England which can take a long time and your Spanish estate should be settled under Spanish law within six months. Having a Spanish will for your Spanish assets will simply speed up the procedure. Of course you must ensure that if you have wills in two different countries they must not contradict each other.

The entire process is potentially complicated and should be discussed with your fiscal advisor or Spanish lawyer. You should keep copies but one word of advice is that these copies should not

Table 3 A simple guide to Spanish tax*

Property tax	*Patrimonio 0.2%* of the property value on the *escritura,* the rateable value or the market value whichever is the higher *Renta* 25% of 1.1% of the rateable value**
Income tax (resident)	After allowances on a sliding scale from 18% to 48% (Note that Spain does not operate PAYE)
Income tax (non-resident) – payable on income in Spain	Flat rate of 25% with no allowances
Wealth tax	For residents after an allowance of €110,000 per person tax begins at 0.2% and rises on a sliding scale For non-residents here is no tax free allowance
Capital gains tax	Residents do not pay CGT on the sale of their main home so long as they reinvest within three years. Those over 65 are exempt from CGT Non-residents are taxed at a flat rate of 35% of the difference between the official buying price of their property and the official selling price
Inheritance tax	Tax depends on the relationship between the deceased and the recipient and after a fixed allowance starts on a sliding scale *This tax is complicated and you should discuss it with your* gestor

* This chart is intended as a guide only. Tax rates and policy change all the time according to the government in power. Please discuss taxes with your *gestor* or, better still, leave the working out of all taxes to him or her

** A resident with only one property is not liable for these taxes but they must be paid on a second property

be held in a bank safe deposit box – should you die in Spain these are sealed for a period following death so no one would be able to access your will and therefore sort out your affairs.

Spanish inheritance laws are very different from those of the UK and an entire book could be written about this topic alone. Unless you really understand the legal aspects it is the one area in which you should take advice.

In the further reading section of this book there are far better sources than this book to help you through the tax maze if you want to do it all by yourself but I would strongly advise the services of a good *gestor* or similar fiscal advisor who really knows the Spanish legal system. You will save yourself considerable hassle.

Summary

- Decide very early whether you want or need *residencia* – legally if you live in Spain for more than six months of the year you should have it but there are many people living here who do not.

- Appoint a fiscal advisor soon after your arrival in Spain – a good fiscal advisor can help tremendously in explaining the mysteries of Spanish legal system to you.

- Sort out your tax situation according to your personal needs.

- Make a Spanish will.

- If you are unmarried but cohabiting, register your relationship with the town hall.

- If you do nothing else, get an NIE number – it will make life much easier. But organise your NIE number through the estate agent through whom you bought the property. You do not need to pay for an NIE number.

- Make your own decision as to whether or not you are going to live legally in Spain.

9 Transport

Wherever you live you need to get around even if it is only to do the normal everyday things. If you currently live in a town or city in the UK, you may be able to walk almost everywhere or there may be a good local bus service should you not want to use your car. Living on the Costa del Sol is not like that. There is almost no area in which you would choose to live where you will have a local bus service every five or ten minutes to take you to local shops and it may even be very difficult to walk to the nearest shopping area.

Should you decide that the area in which you want to settle is Torremolinos or Fuengirola you could have virtually no problems. You might be able to walk to all the shops, bars and restaurants necessary for day-to-day living. You may not need a car and we do know many people who live in these areas who live very well without personal transport. Their only problem happens when they want to visit friends in other parts of the coast who do not have access to the wonderful local public transport system they have locally.

If you choose to live on any other part of the coast or in the inland areas you will almost certainly need your own transport. There will be no alternative.

So what is it like to have a car in Spain?

Should I bring a car from the UK?

Driving around on the Costa del Sol it is amazing how many cars you see with very old British number plates. I often wonder how many of these vehicles are totally legal. Officially, a car with foreign, EU-registered plates should not be driven in Spain for longer than six months in any one year! There are many cars, however, which have been in Spain for far more than six months and they are driven here every day – it is a grey area and it is unlikely to change in the near future. There are many books that state the exact legal situation but equally there are many British expats living here who do not follow these laws and they have had no problems – yet!

It is possible to re-register a car in Spain but to do this you need to have the headlights changed so that they are correct for driving on the righthand side of the road and this can be very expensive. What is vital is that your British-registered car has a valid ITV, the Spanish equivalent of an MOT. Without this document your insurance will be invalid. If the car is on UK plates, an ITV can be granted so long as you have the appropriate black strips on the headlamps, which redirect the beam to the right side of the road. In Spain, an ITV is required every two years after the car is three years old, and when it is ten years old the inspection must be carried out every year. A Spanish ITV will be recognised by most British insurance companies but you should check it out with your own insurance company.

Insurance is vital for any car. There are insurance companies in the UK, on the Costa del Sol or in Gibraltar, who can arrange insurance for a car that is essentially kept outside the UK. When we first moved here we had a UK-registered car. We insured it with a fully comprehensive policy, which was really the equivalent of a permanent green card. In fact we were only allowed to take the car back to the UK for 28 days in any one year without informing the insurance company. It is also a fact of life in the EU that any car must be insured in the country in which it is registered, so if your car is UK-registered it must be insured by a UK-based insurer.

The entire question of car ownership for EU citizens is very difficult when you move from state to state. There are laws that should be obeyed and the majority of individuals do not want to break these laws but the EU bureaucrats have not yet made it easy for the ordinary individual to be a totally law-abiding citizen.

Being legal with your car

As mentioned earlier you should, by law, re-register any car imported from the UK and have it transferred onto Spanish plates after six months. You can only re-register the car if you officially export it from the UK. When your UK MOT expires you cannot pay road tax in the UK because the UK authorities do not recognise the ITV – the Spanish equivalent of the MOT. If you want to be totally legal you cannot pay Spanish road tax because your car is not registered in Spain. Therefore to all intents and purposes you are breaking the law of your adopted country and incidentally you are also breaking the law in the UK.

If you have not officially exported your UK-registered car it will still be registered through DVLA at your UK address – but without road tax. You may find that demands will be sent for payment of the new fine, which is now imposed on individuals who have not paid their road tax, and these demands will be sent to your English address. After all, your UK-registered vehicle is still on the computer at DVLA. Perhaps one solution here is to inform DVLA that the vehicle is no longer being kept on the public roads in the UK. This is, after all, a true statement – it is on Spanish roads.

One point that should be made in this section is that when you move to Spain initially you will not be officially resident here – you will not have *residencia* – but so long as you are non-resident you can still legally drive a UK-registered vehicle. Once you are officially resident in Spain any car – even one imported from the UK – should be re-registered on Spanish plates. A Spanish resident cannot legally drive a car registered in another country. If you apply for *residencia* and continue to drive a UK-registered vehicle you could have problems if you are ever stopped by the police and asked to produce your documents. You may then need to bend the law slightly and show your British passport rather than admitting to having *residencia*.

What is really needed is agreement within the EU on the free movement of cars from one state to another. There is an official position on the free movement of citizens but not yet the free movement of vehicles with all documents recognised and the option to pay road tax in whatever country you live in.

Should I buy a car in Spain?

Yes – and as soon as possible. You will then have no further worries and life will be much simpler!

I would recommend very strongly that as soon as you decide that Spain is where you will live, you sell any UK-registered vehicle you might own and buy a Spanish-registered car. Surprisingly, it is not be too difficult to sell a UK-registered car but when you do this you will immediately be totally legal. You will own a car with the steering wheel on the appropriate side of the vehicle for driving here. The road tax will not only be paid but it is also amazingly low compared to the UK, and your insurance premiums will drop dramatically.

Buying a car

To buy a car in Spain you need to have an NIE number (fiscal number) and proof that you own or rent property in Spain or you will need to have proof of *residencia*. Buying is very simple if you leave the legal details to the dealer from whom you buy the vehicle. There are taxes to pay, which should be included in the selling price, and the vehicle needs to be transferred into your name. The dealer will arrange this. He will organise the registration of your vehicle with the local town hall and all you have to do in the future is to pay the annual road tax. This tax is based on the horsepower of the vehicle and the level is set by the local town hall. In most areas of the Costa del Sol it is low

– very low compared to the UK. The other benefit is that the tax can be paid by direct debit so basically you can forget about it. There are many people who have not paid this tax every year since evidence of payment does not have to be shown on the windscreen. This is false economy since you will have to pay if you ever sell or scrap the car. Not only will you have to pay but you may also have to pay interest charges as well and a fine for non-payment.

The one very real benefit to buying a car locally is that you will probably pay a much lower insurance premium. Car insurance in Spain remains among the cheapest in Europe. We drive a mainstream super-mini and a fully comprehensive insurance policy costs about one third of the premium we would now be paying in London. Our insurance was organised through a major telephone-based insurance company whose logo involves a red telephone bouncing across the TV screen. I will not give them a free commercial by mentioning their name but they are good. More about this in the section on the cost of living.

The other amazing point about Spanish car insurance policies is that they include roadside assistance should your car break down. In the UK such insurance has to be paid for separately through the various well-known and long-established companies who offer this service. This can cost quite a lot of money but when you deduct the cost of this additional policy from your Spanish car policy you realise just how cheap car insurance is here.

So, my advice is that as soon as possible you should buy a Spanish-registered car.

Driving licences

Until you have *residencia* it is perfectly legal to drive in Spain on a UK driving licence. Officially when you become a resident you should apply for a Spanish driving licence which can be applied for at the information desk of the local provincial traffic department (*Jefatura Provincial de Trafico*) within six months of the approval of your *residencia*. You need to produce your UK licence, your residency card and three passport-sized photographs. New EU legislation means that a Spanish licence is no longer mandatory so you do not really need to go through this process but if you are permanently resident in Spain it could be easier to do so.

The old green British driving licence is now only officially valid for tourists and if you still use it you should have a translation in Spanish to accompany the licence.

The other major point about the new EU-style photo card driving licence is that it also works as proof of identity.

Driving in Spain

Car ownership on the Costa del Sol is generally more pleasant than it is in some parts of the UK. The traffic is much lighter and although traffic jams do occur they are never like the jams that you might experience in the SE of England or around major UK cities. I had heard horror stories about the standard of Spanish driving but generally I have to say that there are no problems.

Parking is much easier. The big towns have very adequate and cheap car parks. Many of the smaller towns have not even heard of parking meters and even when they exist the cost of parking is minimal. It is also fascinating to find that in some towns there is no charge for parking during the siesta period – two till five in the afternoon.

The quality of the main roads is very good and when a new road is required it is usually built fairly quickly. However, the quality of side roads can leave a bit to be desired. You also need to consider that your property might be more accessible with a four-wheel drive vehicle. Unlike in the UK, where many such vehicles are status symbols used for the daily school run, on the Costa del Sol they can make the difference between being able to access your property or being stuck in the mud during the rainy season.

There is a remarkable lack of things such as speed cameras along the roadside but occasionally the traffic police do set up radar speed traps. When they do, if stopped for speeding you will be asked to pay a fine, on the spot, in cash. The fines are quite high – the last (and only) time I was stopped I had to pay a fine of almost £100. Drink/driving laws are similar to those in the UK although I have to say that over the years I have lived here I have never heard of anyone being breathalysed. It could happen and you need to be as careful as you would be in the UK. If you are involved in a serious accident and your blood alcohol level is over the limit the Spanish police and courts will throw the book at you. You will probably go to prison and I believe that Spanish prisons are not very pleasant.

Major differences in the laws

There are a few laws in Spain with respect to car ownership and driving which are very different from those in the UK. You should carry the documents relating to your vehicle in the car at all times. Should you be stopped by the police, they will ask to see them. If you are concerned about carrying the original documents it is possible to carry photocopies so long as the copies have been verified at the local notary's office.

New laws also require that if you have to stop after dark as a result of a breakdown you must wear a reflective jacket if you get out of your car. These are now available very cheaply from most supermarkets. Another new law requires you to switch off mobile phones when filling the petrol tank and if you are filling up after dark you should also switch off the lights.

Remember also that if you have *residencia* you should be driving a Spanish-registered car.

Car hire

There are many car hire companies on the Costa del Sol. The major international chains are obviously represented at major airports and railway stations but most towns have their own local car hire companies. Rental costs are very low compared to the rest of Europe particularly out of season when many of the cars may be lying idle. The only negative could be car hire for young drivers. The lower age limit with some companies can be 25 although they are known to make exceptions for established customers.

> The local car hire companies can also be a good source of well-maintained second-hand vehicles since they only keep their cars for 12–18 months and then sell them on at very advantageous prices. Once more, if you buy from the car hire company they will organise the transfer for you.

Public transport

Where it exists, public transport is excellent.

Buses

The bus service is clean, efficient and relatively cheap, the buses are very modern and air-conditioned. The route network is quite extensive. The negative is that they call at every little town and village along the route so journey times can be quite long for what appears to be a relatively short distance. In this respect the service is a bit like the Greyhound service in the US. Unless you live in the centre of a large town it is probably better to have your own transport.

Trains

Train services are limited. There is a metro system in Malaga and there are trains along the coast as far as Fuengirola and north of Malaga along the Guadalhorce river valley. There are plans to extend the train services during the next ten years and when this happens it will then be possible to travel from Estepona to Nerja in 90 minutes. The difference on the Costa del Sol is that this new railway line *will* be built and it *will* open on time. The plans have already been approved. There is also a train service from Algeciras to Malaga or to Granada through the mountains, a very scenic route used a lot by tourists but also a vital lifeline to the mountain communities. Currently the high-speed train line from Madrid is being extended to Malaga and there are longer-term plans to extend it to Estepona.

Taxis

Taxis are very efficient and the wonderful thing here is that there is a price for any journey by taxi, which is set by the Spanish authorities. The drivers have charts that list the prices between the major destinations, so you can ask the price before you make the journey and you know what it will cost in advance. The only additional cost will be motorway tolls should you ask the driver to use the motorway.

Summary

- Decide where you want to live first and then decide whether or not you need a car.

- If you need a car, buy a Spanish-registered car as soon as possible.

- In the longer term it will be better to be totally legal with respect to car ownership. Who knows how EU legislation will change in the future?

- Remember that car insurance on a Spanish-registered car is much cheaper.

- Public transport and taxis are very good where they exist.

10 Healthcare

'What happens if I am ill?' is probably the greatest worry of any new person arriving in Spain. We were worried as well but I hope the following pages will allay any fears you might have.

Will I be healthy in Spain?

It has to be said that you will probably be healthier in Spain than you would be in the UK. The Mediterranean regions in general have a good health record since those who live here tend to eat more fish, fresh fruit and vegetables and use olive oil which many experts reckon is the healthiest oil for cooking or for salads. In addition sensible amounts of red wine have been suggested as a contribution to good health.

The effect of climate

The kind climate also contributes to better health and the warmth of the sun throughout the year probably helps people with rheumatism, arthritis and other connective tissue disorders. There also appears to be a lower incidence of colds and flu-related illnesses and certainly where I am concerned, I find the almost equal distribution of hours of darkness and hours of daylight is much more pleasant in the winter – no more SAD (seasonable affective disorder). It is a proven fact that people react better to life when they have sunlight and with sun for 320 days a year this can only be a positive so long as you do not lie in it too long. This is where the tourist can come a cropper.

The Spanish have one of the highest levels of life expectancy in the EU and this is probably due to the sun, healthy eating habits and a generally laid back attitude to life which removes everyday stress. Many people have said to us that a move to Spain can add years to your life.

Healthcare options

Depending on personal circumstances you have various options when it comes to healthcare provision.

- If you are resident and working in Spain you will have to pay into the Spanish social security system and this will qualify you for entry into the equivalent of the Spanish national health service, INSALUD.

- If you are a retired EU pensioner you automatically qualify for state healthcare so long as you register for it.

- If you are not employed in Spain, outside the social security system and under retirement age you will need private healthcare insurance and you may need to produce evidence of membership of a private scheme in order to obtain *residencia*.

In practice many people who can afford it use a mixture of private and state healthcare and the two systems co-exist quite happily. If only this happened in the UK.

Organising your healthcare

Before you move to Spain you should contact the Pensions and Overseas Benefits Directorate in Newcastle and request an E106 certificate and the relevant forms for you and your family. This provides you with medical cover equivalent to that expected by a Spanish national for a stated period or until you have organised your personal healthcare provision on the Costa del Sol. In our case we had 18 months guaranteed cover at the expense of the NHS should we need to call on it. Cover can be granted for up to two years at the discretion of the NHS.

By the time the certificates expire you should either be in employment in Spain and therefore contributing to Spanish social security or you should have taken out private healthcare for yourself and your family. Until that point the E106 could be a real lifeline. If during that period you become a UK pensioner or the recipient of Incapacity Benefit you may then request another certificate, E121, which will provide you with further medical cover.

State healthcare

If you qualify, the state healthcare system is very good, particularly at hospital level. It is free at the point of use and prescriptions are also free. However, you may be given unbranded (generic) drugs. When entering into the system you need to visit your local social security office and fill in a few forms and produce the documents that prove you are entitled to state healthcare provision. You will then be allocated a doctor at a medical centre near your home for yourself and your family.

If you are retired from the UK or you are registered as disabled you need to obtain a form from the UK social security office, the E121, and take this together with your passport and a copy, *residencia* card (or proof of application), and NIE number. Once more the Spanish social security office will allocate you to a local doctor.

The negatives to the state system are potentially very real. GP surgeries can be very full with long queues and correspondingly long waiting times followed by short appointments with the doctor – much like the UK. The doctors are very well trained but they are under pressure and are more interested in treating the existing condition rather than getting involved in preventative healthcare. In other words, there is a good national illness service. Many of the doctors in the state system may not speak fluent English and this could cause you problems if you do not take along an interpreter. You are also unlikely to find large group practices such as those found in the UK. Many GP practices are single handed with the doctor's wife often working as the receptionist. The UK is also quite unique in having so many practice nurses who spend a lot of time working on prevention rather than cure. You will not find this in Spain.

The other major difference between the Spanish system and the British is that in Spain individual provinces have the decision-making processes on healthcare devolved to a local level. For this reason healthcare standards do vary from province to province but I have to say from personal experience and information from talking to others who live on the Costa del Sol that healthcare here is very good.

Hospitals

When it comes to hospital care the UK is left standing compared to the Costa del Sol. This may be due to the fact that hospitals are jointly funded by the state and by the payments made by the health insurance companies but both types of patient receive equal treatment. The major hospitals are very well equipped, very modern and with state-of-the-art technology. The Costa del Sol Hospital in Marbella probably has one of the best cardiac units in Europe – partly due to an endowment from the Saudi Royal Family who have a 'palace' in Marbella and wanted to ensure their own health. Waiting lists are generally much shorter than in the UK, certainly for the more minor complaints.

Emergency care is second to none and we have only heard praise from patients who have experienced heart emergencies, strokes, cancer and other life threatening conditions. The only negative comments we have heard are that there are too many large meals served in the hospitals!

There are also very good hospitals in Malaga and in Seville with a number of smaller hospitals in other towns. This is however potentially one of the negatives with respect to hospital care on the Costa del Sol. The treatment may be superb but the centre of excellence to which you are sent may not be particularly close to where you live. This can be a problem especially when people want to visit you. One of our friends spent a couple of weeks driving 50 miles each day, each way to Malaga to visit her husband. Not only did this take time but it also cost her a lot on motorway tolls. Similarly another friend's husband is currently being treated for cancer and his centre of excellence for treatment is in Jerez de la Frontera or Seville – a two-hour drive away.

In Spain it is the hospital service that, at the moment, is more interested in preventive medicine – unlike the UK where prevention of illness is now encouraged in general practice. This is a positive aspect of the hospital service but sometimes it can be a little bit too late to start advising on prevention after the illness has developed. One of my friends here who is a Spanish GP in the private sector has commented that preventive medicine must improve in the future in order to save money in the long term. He believes that general practice has to become more involved in preventive medicine and that it will happen.

Private healthcare

If you do not qualify for state healthcare you will need a private insurance policy but this is not as drastic as it might sound. Private healthcare in the UK is very expensive and usually only covers hospital care in private hospitals rather than in state hospitals. Private GP care is almost unheard of in the UK apart from in the expensive areas of large cities. In Spain the public and the private systems work side by side so the actual costs the insurance company may have to pay are probably lower therefore the insurance policies cost much less. As a result more people take out private policies.

In an earlier chapter, which discussed the cost of living, I recounted the fact that my supplier of private health insurance (through my company) invited me to continue the policy when I left the company. The monthly cost was £170. This was in the year 2000 so I shudder to think what it costs now. I declined their offer and returned totally to the state system.

When I arrived in Spain, I contacted various private insurers and finally took out a policy with one company which offers GP cover, hospital cover, emergency ambulance cover and one visit to the dental hygienist every year for about a quarter of that cost. The one thing it does not cover is the cost of prescriptions but generally they are not too expensive. I believe this is very good value for money and if it were available in the UK there would probably be a large number of people who would take up such an option. To be fair this monthly payment will rise by 20% when I reach the age of 60 and when I reach the age of 75 it will not be available but by then I will qualify for free healthcare anyway although I hope I will still be able to afford a visit to see a GP on the private system.

Many of our retired friends who live on the Costa del Sol do consult a GP privately – the costs are quite reasonable – and then fall back on the state system for the necessary treatment. A visit to the GP costs less than a meal for two in an inexpensive restaurant.

Doctors

The benefits to the private option are considerable. There are many doctors from northern European countries as well as Spanish GPs who have trained in other countries who now operate in the private sector, particularly in the larger cities, towns and resort areas and they all speak fluent English. This can make a visit to the doctor much less stressful, even if you speak Spanish.

The other major benefit to using the private sector for GP visits is that since you are paying for the doctor's time and you are given time to discuss why you made the visit in the first place. It is not in and out in ten minutes!

Spain trains more doctors than it needs for the public sector so those doctors who cannot find employment in the state system are perfectly at liberty to set up in private GP practice. Our doctor here is Spanish but after Spanish training he moved to England where he worked in health service hospitals and in British general practice before returning to Spain to set up his own private practice. Private GPs in Spain are also able to advertise their services in the same way as any other professional and as a result there is competition between them which helps to keep the fees charged at an affordable level. Their services are totally professional but since they are running a business they also have to offer a service that the client will buy again.

How private healthcare works

The company I use for healthcare makes it very easy to visit the doctor. I can go to any doctor on their extensive list. They supply me with a booklet of vouchers which I take to the doctor and I simply sign to say that I visited the doctor, he signs to say he treated me and the voucher is sent by him to the company who pay him for his services. Appointments can often be arranged for the same day as you make your telephone call – no more being ill by appointment in a week's time – and when you reach the surgery it is unusual if there is more than one person ahead of you. Usually the person ahead of you is already in consultation with the GP.

The insurance company also issues me with a credit card type identification, which I carry in my wallet so if I am taken to hospital in an emergency the hospital knows that I am covered by health insurance. The same company offers this service in other European countries through reciprocal agreements with other health insurers should I travel outside Spain. It really does provide peace of mind.

Apart from emergency care in hospital which will be provided with questions concerning payment made after treatment, you may be asked for proof of entitlement to state care or private insurance before routine hospital admissions. The identification card from the insurer provides this.

Prescriptions

Prescription costs are not included in the private healthcare policy but this should not frighten anyone accustomed to the UK prescription charge. A course of antibiotics is likely to cost about one third of the UK prescription charge. The same applies to many other routinely used drugs. Basic asthma medication for example is actually available over the counter in the pharmacy without the need for a prescription. If you have asthma and you use salbutamol you can buy this on the Costa del Sol without prescription, without the need to visit the doctor and the cost will be about one third of the cost of a UK prescription.

Other asthma treatments may only be available on prescription and when our GP in Spain wrote a prescription for my partner he did comment that when he worked in the UK he would probably not have been encouraged to prescribe this particular drug.

To the NHS it is considered expensive. In Spain it is a private prescription but the cost is less than that of a pint of beer per day and it has completely controlled his asthma. I wonder how many people in the UK would be prepared to pay this, given the choice, for the real clinical benefit but unfortunately the one thing which the NHS does not allow is a mix of public and private medicine – Spain does. There is no postcode prescribing in Spain.

Medical records

The only negative I can see to long-term healthcare in Spain is the fact that your medical records at the moment have to stay in the UK. They belong to the NHS. Our records for example are still held by the surgery we used in SW London. Luckily our medical histories are fairly simple so our Spanish GP does not have too many problems in dealing with our medical care but when I discussed this situation with him as a potential treatment complication, he did say that there have been instances where problems have occurred when treating expatriates with complex medical histories when the records have not been immediately available. Some of these situations could even be life threatening.

However, the law in the UK now allows you access to your medical records and before you leave the UK you can ask your current surgery for a synopsis of your personal records which you can then take to any doctor who might treat you on the Costa del Sol. There may be a charge for the supply of this information. You must also take into consideration that when you register with a Spanish doctor he/she cannot request your records from your former UK GP on your behalf. This differs from the situation of moving from one part of the UK to another and registering with a new doctor. If your medical history is at all complicated you should request this summary before you leave the UK since it could make your future medical treatment easier.

Emergency care

Wherever you live in the world there is always the worry about how soon emergency services will arrive when you need to call them.

The ambulance service on the Costa del Sol is not always a part of the service operated by your nearest hospital. If you are an EU citizen you should qualify for emergency care in terms of ambulances but you might find that you have to pay up front and then claim the cost back from the authorities and you also need to know which telephone number to call.

The Red Cross (*Cruz Rioja*) are very involved and have a prominent presence but if you need to call them you may also be asked to pay for immediate service and they do not always speak fluent English. This could be a problem in a life-threatening emergency.

If you have private health insurance they will provide ambulance service, which can be called upon in an emergency, and the insurance company will provide you with the appropriate telephone number. You can also choose to pay an annual subscription to a private emergency service.

The definitive emergency service

We are very lucky on the Costa del Sol to have what I consider to be the definitive emergency healthcare system – *Helicopteros Sanitarios*.

For not much more than £1.00 per week per person (even less for a family policy), this service offers superlative emergency healthcare. In fact they advertise as 'your 24 hour home doctor'. The company covers the coast and the immediate inland area from Torremolinos to Sotogrande. If you have to call, an intensive care road ambulance will arrive, usually within half an hour, with an English-speaking doctor and a nurse. This ambulance is virtually a mobile hospital equipped with ECG monitors, oxygen, defibrillators and emergency medication. Treatment will be offered on the spot with a follow up prescription for additional medication but if the medical team consider that hospitalisation is necessary they will either take you to the nearest local hospital by road or call in the services of their emergency helicopter service.

If you feel unwell you can telephone 24 hours a day and they will treat you in your own home. It must also be said that early treatment at home often prevents the real emergency happening. The company offering this service do not see themselves purely as an emergency service but rather as a mobile GP service.

Anyone can join this amazing service. There is no upper age limit, penalties or exclusion clauses because of medical history and you can call them out as often as necessary. Should you have to call them your medical history is then entered on their computer and future calls will result in the medical team being fully briefed on your medical history before they even arrive in your home. If they have to transfer you to hospital the hospital will also be briefed in advance on your history and told of any allergies, current daily medication, chronic conditions or indeed any other relevant factors which could affect your treatment. If necessary they will also organise your transfer from one hospital to another.

We know people who experienced a heart attack or a stroke who called *Helicopteros Sanitarios*. Within 30 minutes of the initial call they were on their way to intensive care facilities in hospital. Indeed if the initial call suggests to the operator that this is the emergency situation the first contact will probably be by helicopter.

I would suggest that there are very few places, if any, in the UK today where you would expect or receive such a rapid service following an emergency call. *Helicopteros* are so well organised that they provide you with stickers for your car windscreen so that should the emergency services have to rescue you from your car the first point of contact will be this service. They also offer the same service whether you are on the beach, on the golf course or indeed anywhere and when you ring them there will always be an operator who speaks fluent English. Membership of this service takes away all the worries about emergency healthcare in a foreign country. Emergency healthcare on the Costa del Sol is therefore *Helicopteros Sanitarios*.

Since the service is so successful, the company is now expanding and is now able to offer add on services at additional cost. These services cover annual health checks, convalescent care and even long term nursing care.

The pharmacy *(La Farmacia)*

As in many other European countries the first point of call for minor ailments has to be the pharmacy. Pharmacists in Spain are highly trained and are very skilled in recommending therapies which will deal with everyday ailments and save you a visit to your doctor. Pharmacists are very proud of their professional services. Pharmacies in Spain only sell prescription drugs or those drugs which in the UK can only be sold through a registered pharmacist.

The Spanish pharmacy is not the shop you visit to buy toiletries, shampoos, or all the other things which high street pharmacies sell in the UK. The pharmacies on the Costa del Sol are very professional retail outlets which can be of immense help to you should you have a minor health problem. Should your Spanish not be totally proficient, you will find that there will be someone in the pharmacy, at least in the coastal areas, who speaks English and who will be able to advise you on appropriate medication or who might suggest that you really should consult a doctor. The pharmacist is also in the position to recommend a suitable doctor.

Before you move to Spain you should note the official names of any medicines you take regularly or those in which you have complete confidence. The official name is often referred to as the generic name and this will be recognised by your Spanish pharmacist (or GP) even if the local brand name is different. For example, a well-known painkiller in the UK is Nurofen but the generic name for this drug is Ibuprofen. The pharmacist in Spain will recognise this name and be able to provide you with a local equivalent even if the brand name differs.

The E111

What you should not do – but what many people continue to do – is to use the UK E111 form as a guarantee of healthcare cover in Spain. This form is intended to provide a British citizen with emergency healthcare while on holiday in another EU country. There are many individuals who actually live in Spain who continue to use the E111 as their source of local healthcare provision. They can do this because they still have an official UK address even although they may not actually live there. It is possible that this loophole could be closed in the future through stricter controls since it is actually illegal. In reality if any of these individuals who use the E111 are retired EU pensioners they should request the E121 form from their local social security office in the UK. Younger families should either register with Spanish social security or take out private health insurance.

Alternative medicine and therapies

These are also well catered for on the Costa del Sol. Reference to the local equivalent of the *Yellow Pages* will provide you with contacts for chiropractors, masseurs, chiropodists, osteopaths and many other practitioners of alternative therapies. Treatment will be private but because of the differences in the relative costs of living you will find that the treatment should cost you considerably less than it might do in the UK.

Long-term medical care

It is possibly in this area where Spain is less well equipped than the UK. In this country it has been traditional for the family to look after their elderly relatives so there are far fewer residential old people's homes on the Costa del Sol than you would find on the south coast of England. The situation is changing as developers realise that there is an ageing expatriate population and many have the resources to move into what we would call sheltered accommodation but it is still slow to develop. This is potentially a growth industry and yet another way to sell property so there will be more facilities in the future.

There are also fewer hospices and other facilities for the care of the terminally ill on the Costa del Sol. Once more the family has been expected to look after such cases. This is also changing but it will take time.

There is also less provision for convalescent care. You must realise that in Spain it is expected that patients convalesce at home, looked after by their family. As a result patients tend to spend less time in hospital after an operation.

As mentioned earlier however the emergency service *Helicopteros Sanitarios* can now organise personalised convalescent or long term nursing care at additional cost.

Dentistry

There is no shortage of English-speaking dentists in the various coastal towns of the Costa. Many of these dentists are English, Scandinavian, Dutch or German and have set up private practices here. The quality of dentistry is identical to that you would expect in the UK but once more the relative costs of living mean that it will cost you much less than you might expect. In fact the price you might expect to pay in the UK in pounds is the price you will pay here in Euros which effectively means that dentistry is 40% cheaper in real terms.

Dentists can advertise their services so to all intents and purposes they are running a commercial business and the prices charged must therefore be competitive to attract business to the practice.

Dentistry, apart from the services of the dental hygienist, is not normally covered on health insurance.

Should you require the services of a dentist it is better to find a high street dentist rather than the dentist who is operating a practice in one of the franchises in a large department store or hypermarket. These dentists are primarily catering for the tourist population who do not know where to find the best local dentists and as a result their charges are often much higher and may even be similar to UK prices.

Opticians

Optical services are just as well developed as they are in the UK but what does not yet appear to have reached the Costa del Sol is the large chain store approach to selling spectacles as fashion accessories. In every town or city you will find local opticians and if you ask the locals you will be able to find opticians who speak English because once more it can be much easier to take an eye test if you understand the questions. Despite the absence of the large chains of optical stores the cost of new glasses is not high on the Costa del Sol and the choice of frames is just as good as you would expect in the UK.

Summary

- Spain has a healthy climate and a healthy population.

- Organise temporary cover for you and your family through the E106 before you leave the UK.

- If you plan to live in Spain do not consider that the E111 is your passport to long term healthcare.

- Before you leave the UK ask for a summary of your medical records from your current GP.

- If you work in Spain you will have to contribute to Spanish social security and this will provide healthcare.

- If you are self-employed or semi-retired and under retirement age, consider private healthcare.

- Even if you are covered by the state, consider private healthcare if you can afford it.

- Sign up to one of the emergency healthcare companies.

- Regard the pharmacy as a valuable health resource.

- Do not worry about dentistry, optical care or sources of alternative medicine – they are all here at very competitive prices.

11 Education

For younger families relocating to Spain, the education of their children is a very important consideration. Depending on the age of your children you have various options in either state or private schools.

Learning options

The state system

If you have very young children and you intend to stay on the Costa del Sol permanently then it is probably very sensible to enrol them in the nearest Spanish state school. Early immersion in the Spanish language will ensure that your children should grow up bilingual and it is also true to say that children learn another language very quickly. If you follow this approach you will be giving your children the opportunity to leave school able to speak two of the most commonly spoken languages in the world.

For the child who does not speak Spanish at the time of enrolment some state schools (but not all) on the Costa del Sol offer tuition in the Spanish language – check with the school of your choice. State schools offer free education according to the Spanish curriculum. Every village, town or city has its own state schools and I could not even begin to list them. Suffice to say that many parents do choose the state system for practical reasons or quite simply because they cannot afford private education. Wherever you move to, the first step will be to identify people locally who have moved from the UK and ask them questions about education and where to find the best schools.

A mixture of state and private education

Some parents approach the question of education from a different perspective. They enrol their children in the state system for primary education and when the time comes for secondary education they switch to the private sector in an international school. Using this approach the child becomes fluent in Spanish but when the time comes for moving to the next level they can then follow a UK or international type curriculum.

The private sector

A third route which many parents may choose to follow if their children are older is to put them straight into private education in an international school which follows a similar curriculum to that the child was already following in the UK. This prospect is not as daunting as it seems since many international schools are much less expensive than their equivalents back in the UK. Private education remains affordable in Spain.

University entrance

The final question that many parents will ask is what happens when it comes to university entrance? Once more there is no real problem. If your children have been educated in the Spanish state system they will leave school with qualifications which will be recognised by most universities around the world. If they have attended an international school there will be no problem whatsoever but of course if they have Spanish qualifications and speak fluent Spanish there are many excellent universities in Spain and if you have resident status in Spain, bursaries are available for university education. Spanish universities are still state-run and grants are available for Spanish residents according to the income of the parents.

Any doubts about mutual recognition of school leaving qualifications should you want your children to go back to the UK to a British university can be dealt with by contacting the British Council or NARIC in the UK, either of whom can give you information about mutual recognition of qualifications. Both organisations can be accessed on the Internet.

So what is the situation regarding education in Spain under the various options?

State education

Schooling in Spain is co-educational but remains very formal in terms of the teaching style. It is provided free of charge, and it now ranks alongside Europe's best, so you should have no worries if your children are educated in a state school on the Costa del Sol. Between the ages of 6 and 16 education is compulsory and Spanish parents are all now very determined that their children will have a good education.

Pre-primary, there are state schools available and these are also free. (They are supplemented by fee-paying pre-primary school education should you wish to follow this route.) The only potential problem with Spanish pre-primary school education is the very formal attitude that is still in place. The children may not be allowed to follow the 'self-expression' form of teaching which is now normal in the UK. They will sit behind a desk and be taught very formally. Such schools prepare children for the educational procedures that follow during the compulsory period of education.

Beyond the age of 16 state schools are available that will allow your children to proceed to the *bachillerato,* which is an additional two free years of education which should result in an entrance qualification for university. This qualification is generally recognised worldwide.

Examinations

One potential negative to British parents is that, in the state system, annual examinations are still considered to be very important and if children do not pass these exams they could be held back for a further year until they do pass. This is very similar to the educational system I followed in Scotland in the 1960s and it is the way that the state system still functions in Spain.

Vocational training

One thing that remains important in the Spanish state system is a continuing emphasis on vocational training. The Spanish still recognise the fact that not all children will progress – or indeed want to – to university and it is therefore important that pupils are given a grounding in clerical work, electronics, design and all the other things which are an important part of modern life and society. This is absolutely wonderful for those students who may not be academically inclined and really sets them up for a vocation in life.

University

With all the publicity surrounding university fees in the UK over the last few years it is a sobering fact that only about a quarter of Spanish students actually go on to university but it is probably the case that only a quarter actually want to progress through this route. Throughout the educational process in Spain there is always the possibility that students can switch between the more academic programme with the long-term view of university entrance or the more practical programme of vocational training. Needless to say there is no real difference between a university education in Spain and a similar education anywhere else in the EU. While still at school even those students who follow a vocational route can still switch over to the *bachillerato* should they decide this is the way forward. All they need to do is to take additional specialist training and pass the relevant exams.

A possible negative about state education is the fact that with the increasing number of foreign residents living in Spain, many of whom have chosen the state route, class sizes are getting bigger. The state system has not always bargained for the increase in the number of students because new residents have not always registered at the local town hall. This is one more example of local infrastructure not keeping up with the local demand that new residents make on it because the authorities either do not know that we are here (unlikely) or can claim that we are not here because we have not registered.

University education in Spain varies from three-year courses which are essentially vocational – teaching or nursing type courses following which the student receives a *diplomado* (diploma) – through to five-year courses from which the student emerges with a qualification which would be the UK equivalent of an MSc or comparable degree in the UK (*licenciado*). At the moment, university education for residents of Spain is free for those students who can demonstrate that they would benefit from university education and are therefore awarded a scholarship or bursary. The courses differ from those offered in the UK and they can be longer, which is why many Spanish students do tend to go abroad to study at university (if they can afford it).

International schools

Many parents opt for private education in Spain since they prefer to have their children educated according to an international curriculum based largely on the British system. They feel confident that their children will leave school with qualifications that are recognised around the world for university entrance.

There are many private, international schools all along the Costa del Sol and many of them are very affordable. Obviously, the choice depends on where you live and how convenient the school will be for your children. It is vital that you check the prospectus of any schools under consideration. Many are run as businesses and may even be owned by the headmaster. They may promise a class size of 15 but your child may end up in a class much bigger than this simply because more children have been accepted into the school because at the end of the day each child is a revenue source. If parents complain they may be told that if they do not like the system they can take their children elsewhere.

As you get closer to Malaga there will probably be a greater choice, which can be a real benefit because increased competition can reduce the fees. Reference to Internet sites during the preparation of this book suggested that annual fees in this part of the coast can be between €3,200 and €5,500 for primary (the lower figure) to secondary education.

However, even at the western end of the Costa del Sol, one of the most prestigious schools in the area only charges between €4,100 and €9,300 depending on the age of the child. This is in a school where the pupil count is 630 and the teacher count is 67! How many schools in the UK can offer one teacher to every 10 children? The only negative is that there can be quite a high turnover of teachers since many only stay on the coast for two or three years.

A typical school

Having downloaded the information from the Internet about the school mentioned above, the details are quite astonishing compared to the average UK school. The buildings are all new. There is a central learning centre, which has a theatre, a multimedia library, a computer suite, art and music studios and a cafeteria. There are wireless communication links throughout the school, which means that the students can access the Internet or the school's own intranet. There are wonderful sports facilities including a 25-metre swimming pool and a sports pitch and running track. Great emphasis is put on outdoor activities.

Secondary students in this school follow a curriculum that is based on the best features of the English, Spanish and European curricula, and students can leave with the International General Certificate of Secondary Education (IGCSE) and GCSE qualifications. Students who stay on for a further two years can take the International Baccalaureate Diploma. This qualifies the holder for entry to most of the world's best universities.

One minor point worth noting about this school is the fact that it supplies school buses to transport the children to school from a very wide catchment area. In fact, school buses remain an important fact of general school life in Spain in both the private and state sector all along the coast. The 'school run' by individual mothers is not such an institution on the Costa del Sol.

Further reference to the Web site for this school shows that they have a very high success rates at all levels of exams.

I would not presume to know the situation with all the private sector schools on the Costa del Sol but I do know this school and many of the students who attend it. Without exception, both parents and children are more than satisfied. The potential benefits to some parents is the knowledge that in an international school their children will be educated in English as well as being taught Spanish, so once more they should leave school bilingual.

For parents who are interested in international schools a simple search on the Internet for international schools, Costa del Sol, will provide a list of schools that can be selected according to the part of the coast in which you live. Most schools now have their own Web sites. Parents should make their own decisions. A list of schools is provided in Appendix 5.

There are, of course, also Spanish schools in the private sector. These schools actually attract a state subsidy but they do follow the Spanish curriculum and teaching will be in Spanish.

How children react

I have heard only positive comments from parents on the Costa del Sol when they talk about their children's education. The schools appear to be much better than the majority of schools in the UK. The classes are generally smaller. There still appears to be quite a high level of school discipline. Children still wear school uniform. Most schools do provide very good extra-curricular activities and the children all seem to be very happy. I know families who have moved here with their children and on the first day the children were very concerned about going to a new school but by the end of the first day they could not wait to go back to school the following day.

Younger children learn the language very quickly and soon they may even be teaching their parents Spanish. Children become the interpreters for their parents on occasions. Therefore young children could benefit tremendously from entry into the Spanish state system at least for primary education. After primary education only you can make the decision as to how you want your child to be educated at secondary level.

Older children may have more problems in learning Spanish to the level adequate for their educational needs so older children who have relocated from the UK may be better off placed in an international school where they will be taught in English but given the opportunity to learn Spanish as a second language.

Table 4 School education

Level	Options	Age group	State* (qualifications)	Private (qualifications)
Pre-school	Voluntary	1–6		
Primary	Compulsory	6–12		
Secondary	Compulsory	12–16	(Graduate in Secondary Ed)	(IGCSE)
Secondary	Voluntary	16–18	(Bachillerato**)	(A/S or A Level or International Baccalaureat
	Vocational	16–18	Vocational Diploma	

* Note that in Spanish state schools education is divided into two two-year cycles and failure to pass all examinations at the end of the first two years requires the pupil to repeat a year and be re-examined. This situation is under review

** Accepted for university entrance

Whatever decisions you make as a parent, I believe that your children could benefit tremendously from education on the Costa del Sol. They will achieve qualifications that equal those from any other European country and will provide access to universities around the world. They should leave school able to speak two languages fluently. They will also have been immersed in a European culture with all the benefits that that will provide in their future lives. If they wish to progress to university they can then decide whether they want to go to university in an English-speaking country or in Spain.

In fact, children often seem to adjust to a new life on the Costa del Sol even more rapidly than their parents so education should not be a worry for parents who want to move their children here. The children will benefit!

Table 5 Post-school education – the options

Education type	Age	State or private	Qualification
University	18–21	Grant-aided state university	Licenciado*
University	18–23	Grant-aided state university	MSc (equivalent) Diplomado**
Foreign university or college (e.g. UK)	18–21	Fee paying (UK)	UK degree (depends on subject)

* Nurses, chemists, pharmacists

** Doctors, lawyers, architects, engineers

Summary

- Spanish state education is the equal of any in Europe.

- The public sector and the private sector live happily together.

- Young children learn Spanish very quickly and could benefit from entry into the state system.

- Older children might be better off in an international school.

- Private education in Spain is much less expensive than it is in the UK.

- Check the prospectus of selected schools before committing your child to that school.

- In the private sector the teacher/pupil ratio is usually very positive.

- Educational qualifications are now internationally recognised.

- Educating your children in Spain should result in them being bilingual when they leave school.

- The ability to speak both languages fluently means that your children could go to university in Spain.

12 Working on the Costa del Sol

Now that we all live in the European Community it is possible for British citizens to work in Spain under the same legal conditions as the local population. You can find a job on the Costa del Sol even before you have *residencia* but you do need to have an NIE number to work here legally.

The job market

The job market is not easy and Spain does have quite a high rate of unemployment – one of the highest in the EU – but job opportunities have changed dramatically. Several years ago it would have been almost impossible to find a job unless you spoke fluent Spanish. As a result many new arrivals from northern Europe were forced to accept very low-paid jobs, usually in the catering industry, if they needed to work to make ends meet. This has changed with the increase in the number of foreign residents who now live here. There are jobs available even for those who do not speak Spanish. Most of these jobs are with companies who are servicing the needs of the expatriate community. There are also many opportunities for entrepreneurs to set up their own businesses offering services that the expats need, and later I will describe some of these potential opportunities.

Job centres

When you first arrive you have six months to look for work. It is possible to sign on at the local job centre, the INEM (*Instituto Nacional de Empleo* – telephone number in your local telephone directory). If you take this approach it is a very good idea to have your CV translated into Spanish. Should the INEM find you work you have the right to the Spanish minimum wage and if you are offered a temporary position you can only be given two temporary contracts of three sequential months each or one contract for six months after which your employer has to give you, by law, a permanent contract.

Many employers however will terminate the first contract after three months and leave a gap of several weeks (you are offered a holiday!) before offering a second contract and by doing this they do not have to offer a permanent contract. Contracts have to be sequential in order for the law to be followed!!

When you start work in Spain you will be liable for Spanish income tax but you need to realise that Spain does not yet operate a PAYE scheme. You have to pay your income tax in several instalments throughout the course of the year and currently if you earn more than €8,000 a year you must, by law, fill in a tax return. Once more your *gestor* can do this for you.

Social security

When you work in Spain the law also demands that you should pay contributions to the Spanish social security system. This will cover you for state healthcare and unemployment benefit. Pension benefits do not start until you have 15 years of contributions. If you are self-employed the total contribution is payable by you and it can be as high as 30% of your income. If you are employed by a company the payments are shared between the employee and the employer with the latter paying a higher amount. The employee only pays around 6%. Should you ever need to claim unemployment benefit you can only do so if you have worked for 360 days during the last six years and you have to register with the INEM within 15 days of losing your job.

Official holiday entitlement is quite generous in Spain. Everyone is entitled to 23 days' annual holiday plus national and local public holidays.

The official job market in Spain is governed by EU law and if you do find a job through official channels you will be liable for income tax and social security payments but you will have the protection granted by employment law to employees. Having said this it is quite common for foreigners who are running their own businesses here to pay staff in cash leaving their staff to take personal care of all the appropriate payments (many do not). The benefit to the employers is that they are not responsible for the employment on-costs such as the employer's contribution to social security.

Working without an employment contract

There are many people who are prepared to work here without an official contract of employment. This is illegal but in the past many have accepted it without question since they needed the work. However, the authorities are now starting to tighten up on the regulations and it is quite likely that in future they will toughen up their stance on these 'illegal' employers. Remember, you are entitled to a contract of employment under EU law and the contract should cover the salary offered, the period for salary reviews, working hours, social security payments, holiday entitlement and the policy of the company with regard to dismissal and redundancy.

Newly-arrived inhabitants on the Costa del Sol have accepted poor working conditions, lack of official contracts and low wages for too long but at the end of the day it is up to the individual to decide what he/she is prepared to accept.

What are your options?

If you really want to succeed in the search for employment on the Costa del Sol, it will help if you speak Spanish. This will open the door to so many more opportunities and should you speak a third language your opportunities will be even greater. With a command of languages you could find work with companies whose business is targeted to the many foreign residents on the Costa del Sol.

Without fluent Spanish your options are more limited, but they exist, particularly in the coastal areas where most potential work will be allied to the needs of the expat community.

The service industries

There is bar work or restaurant work but this is likely to be paid in cash and the hourly rate might be very low. Your employer will probably not pick up the costs of social security and the work may also be seasonal. When the business is not busy you will not have a job but the employer will be happy to welcome you back when the tourists arrive again. Similarly other service industries offer regular, if not terribly glamorous, jobs. There is a constant need for cleaners to maintain the many second homes that exist on the coast. There is also a need for gardeners, pool cleaners and caretakers with basic maintenance skills.

Engineers and mechanics

There are also good opportunities for engineers and mechanics who are skilled in the servicing of upmarket vehicles. We know of people with such skills who have found work with local garages within days of arriving on the coast.

Building workers

If you have painting and decorating experience, plumbing, building, carpentry or similar skills there is potentially a lot of work available particularly from non-Spanish speaking expats who want to use the services of tradesmen to whom they can describe the required job without any language problems. Many people who have moved here are using these skills to make a comfortable living. Many offer their services as part of the 'black' economy and are paid in cash. This is fine, but if you really want to succeed in this type of employment in the long term, you should consider setting up your own official company. After all, the really lucrative contracts could come from people who want to renovate a large property and who want VAT receipts to justify their expenditure and therefore reduce their liability for capital gains tax when they sell.

If you speak fluent Spanish and you have a background in the building industry there are very good opportunities to offer your services as a project manager for restoration or general building projects. If you are able to communicate fully with the local builders you will be able to offer your clients a very good service through your contacts with local tradesmen who will probably charge a lot less for the work than the expat offering the same service. After all, if the local contractor is able to offer a lower hourly rate, the rate to your client will still look very competitive even after the addition of your commission to the bill and the work done will be totally legitimate.

The professions

If you possess recognised professional qualifications you might find that these are recognised, or can be recognised, in Spain so you could open a business as a vet, an optician, a dentist, or a practitioner of alternative medicine. If you have a medical or legal qualification this might also open the door to practising on the Costa del Sol with your own private practice although you might need to obtain some additional Spanish qualifications. You do need to check whether your qualifications are recognised under Spanish/EU law. You should be able to do this through your professional society, through the Spanish Consulate in the UK, NARIC or through EU Web sites. There is not the space in this book to go through all the various professions.

Estate agents

Unlike many other European countries the estate agency market in Spain is not yet governed by a huge number of regulations and there are many people working in Spain in real estate without any background or qualifications. I have never met so many estate agents in my life or those who think they are estate agents. With a booming property market many are making a very good living indeed but I have to say that this is a very competitive market and your income may depend very heavily on how many properties you actually sell. If you are happy with the hard-sell approach it would be a possibility for employment – you will probably have a contract of employment but most of your income could be in the form of commission. My only reservation about this area of work would be that, in the longer term, Spain may introduce some of the more stringent regulations which already exist in other European countries concerning estate agents. This could change this potential employment opportunity dramatically.

At the moment the potential rewards are high but should you choose this route you could end up with a seven-day-a-week job with very long hours and very high sales targets, particularly in the summer months when there are many potential viewers of property for sale.

Jobs in this sector are heavily advertised in the English-language press. Some involve selling property while others are in the timeshare-selling business, which is even more aggressive.

Finding work

Until fairly recently the most common way for jobs to be filled in Spain was through word of mouth. Many jobs, particularly those available to the local population, were found through family or friends and this may still be the case in many rural areas. Even for the expat this can still be a very good way of finding employment if you have good networking skills and have access to a wide circle of friends or acquaintances – many of whom might know of work opportunities.

The large number of English-language newspapers and magazines on the Costa del Sol do carry quite large situations vacant adverts and these are obviously targeted at the expat population – their readership. Many of these vacancies, although targeted at native English speakers, do ask for the ability to speak Spanish so once more you really need to learn the language. Many of the positions on offer are office-based and many are in the property sector or telesales but there are also many positions in the IT industry, which is currently a real growth area on the Costa del Sol. It has to be said that there are not many high-paid, professional or managerial jobs advertised in the pages of these publications.

A new development on the coast is the introduction of employment agencies. Traditionally Spanish companies have been reluctant to use the services of agencies but they are starting to do so. This may be a solution in finding work for better-qualified people in the future. One employment agency was quoted recently in a local publication as stating that the one positive factor here is that there does appear to be less ageism. Well-qualified individuals in their 40s or 50s can find work since many employers recognise the potential benefits of experience. Local employment agencies advertise in the English-language press but you must check them out for yourself. I have not used them so it would be wrong for me to recommend anyone in particular.

Working in Gibraltar

As mentioned earlier, another possibility for work on the Costa del Sol if you live at the western end is to search for employment opportunities in Gibraltar. There are employment agencies in Gibraltar, or you could ask friends to get you a copy of the *Gibraltar Chronicle* so that you can check out what is available. The benefits to working there is that it is (officially) British. The language is officially English so if you do not speak Spanish there might not be the same problem.

If you are employed in Gibraltar you will pay your tax there and you will be included in the local social security system but this will mean that you will have to consult doctors in Gibraltar or should you need hospital care you will also need to go there. Since Gibraltar is a major centre for financial operations, individuals with banking or finance experience might find it easier to find work. There is also a booming shopping area since the colony is a duty-free shopping centre. As a result, shop work is probably available.

The negative to working in Gib if you live in Spain is simply getting to work every morning. The queue to enter the colony can be very long and it can be even longer to get back out again. In fact, most people who go to Gibraltar every day find somewhere to park in Spain, in La Linea, and they then walk across the border every day and use the bus to the town centre.

Self-employment

A very common solution to employment needs for many people who relocate to the Costa del Sol is to set up their own business, capitalising on skills learned in the UK. It is a growth area and is often encouraged by local government authorities who recognise that new businesses which may end up employing the local population are to be encouraged. If your new business plays a part in encouraging tourism and therefore the influx of more money into the area, you will find local government supportive.

Many individuals who do set up businesses do however tailor their activities to the expatriate market and even here there is no shortage of potentially successful business ideas. Many new ventures are targeted to the leisure or catering market or to property sales or management.

Do your market research

The first step is to conduct the appropriate market research to establish that there is a real need for the business you intend to open in your area. Assuming there is, you must then take the correct legal advice to make sure that your proposals are legal and that you understand all the financial implications.

If you can find an established business, which is being sold as a going concern, and the reason for the sale is genuine this could be a very wise move. You must, however, look very carefully into the reasons for the sale. You need to check that there are no local plans that could seriously affect long-term success and, most important of all, you need to check that there are no outstanding bills. In Spain the bills go with the business and will be automatically transferred to you.

You should also check that all the necessary licences for your proposed venture actually exist if the business requires a licence. These could include the original Opening Licence, the Municipal Licence and Business Licence and the licence for the serving of food if you are proposing to run a restaurant or bar. If you buy existing premises and run them exactly as they were there is less problem with the opening licence but if you change the nature of the business you need a new licence.

If you are proposing to run an operation that is dependent on your professional qualifications you also need to check that these are valid in Spain. Clear all these hurdles and you could well be on your way to a successful future as a self-employed person on the Costa del Sol. Ignore some or all of them and you could be on the way to financial ruin and the end of your dream of a new life in the sun.

So, what sort of businesses do people open on the coast and how successful can they be?

Self-employment options

Bars and restaurants

There are many people who have had a personal dream of running a bar or a restaurant in the sun and they have been featured in many reality television programmes. Some have been very successful but for every successful catering establishment there are probably many more which have ruined their owners financially or personally. The hours, especially in the height of the tourist season, can be very long. Some bars are open until very late in the night. The competition is fierce and if you are dependent mainly on tourist business, there is virtually no customer loyalty. The punters will go to the bar they like best during their holiday but they may never be back again. Next year they will visit another resort probably in another country!

On the coast the average restaurant in the summer months will be open until one or two in the morning and then be open again for lunch the next day, seven days a week. In season you cannot afford to close even for a day since the potential customer may go elsewhere and stick with the other restaurant. You will almost certainly need to employ staff to help you run the business and legally this should involve you in social security payments for your staff unless you employ them illegally.

Catering businesses, which are dependent on the tourist trade, can also suffer if business drops as a result of world events. In 2003 the Iraq War virtually destroyed the Easter trade on the Costa del Sol – no-one was travelling – although it picked up by the summer as a result of late bookings. In 2004 the Madrid bombs and the strong dollar adversely affected tourism in Spain.

There will almost certainly be increasing interference from the EU with new directives on the running of bars and restaurants. This could cost you a lot of money in the future or might even result in your premises being closed. There has been a tradition in Spain of not following all the directives to the letter whereas in the UK they are followed stringently. Sighting of a cockroach near or in a restaurant in the UK would probably result in the place being closed by the Health and Safety inspectors – just think what a client would make of a sighting of a cockroach in your restaurant!

I have experienced cockroaches walking over my feet here in some restaurants.

There is no question that a well-run, successful and fashionable bar or restaurant in the right area can be very successful on the Costa del Sol but it is more likely to fall into this category if you already have experience in running such an establishment in the UK. Bars and restaurants are not a hobby – they are really hard work.

The above also applies to the possibility of opening a nightclub or a discotheque. If you have a track record in this very competitive business you could be successful. If instead it has always been your dream to be a nightclub proprietor you could lose your life savings very quickly. Unless you are in the right area with a club that everyone wants to visit because it is fashionable, life could be difficult.

Guest houses, bed and breakfast and holiday lets

This is another area where many people have had dreams of opening a successful business. Once more a well-run establishment can be a good source of income but it can also be a very rapid way to take you into bankruptcy. If you have sufficient capital to allow you either to buy a well-modernised and successful business without a large mortgage it is worth considering. If the property you buy needs extensive modernisation before you can open it as a guest house you need to be more careful. The renovation work will almost certainly cost more than you bargained for and if you have to borrow the money to do it you then need to be able to recoup that investment by letting the rooms on a very regular basis.

Your income will not be terribly high. If you go on the Internet and look at B&B accommodation on the Costa del Sol you might be very surprised to see that even well-modernised premises are only generating an income of €50 to €70 per night for a double room – and that is a premium rate – others are much cheaper. In your first year you need to budget for a relatively low room-occupancy rate – 20 to 30% average occupancy could be realistic. Once your establishment is well-known you might achieve a much higher rate of occupancy. If you build up a very good reputation you might be able to charge higher room-rates because you are nearly always full but you should not bargain on this during the first few years.

There is also a relatively low demand for guesthouse accommodation on the coast itself. Most visitors to the coast are after the sun, sea and sangria and will rent an apartment or stay in a budget hotel or they will be here on a package holiday. Guesthouse demand is mainly in the inland areas for rural tourism generated by independent travellers but if your dream property is situated in an inland village or town it might be very unusual for guests to stay with you for more than two or three days before they move on to another destination. Local government is however very ready to talk to individuals who have plans for rural tourism projects.

Rural tourism

Rural tourism is an important future growth area but it is vital that you do not overstretch yourself in terms of loans to achieve your dream unless you really do your homework and your market research very carefully. Only by doing this will you be able to forecast what your long term return might be and it could be a long-term return. The rural tourism market is not the same market as the traditional market for the sunseeker on the Costa del Sol and to be really successful it will require much more marketing not just from you but also from local government.

A change in mindset is necessary. We know many people who have visited this part of Spain to explore the inland areas and they have loved it but it would be wrong for me to say that this is the first impression that the average person has of the Costa del Sol. It has been generally perceived as a beach resort area or a golfing area.

Holiday rentals

Holiday lets are another area where the dream you have may not actually become a reality. Many people buy 'investment' properties with a view to letting them for up to half the year. Indeed, many developers sell new properties with part of the sales pitch being the potential return on rental. Some developers even 'guarantee' rental income. How can they do this unless they have the clients who want to rent the property?

This was the situation a few years ago but now the large number of properties under construction could result in oversupply making it difficult to rent your property for the number of weeks you have budgeted for in your initial calculations especially if these calculations involve the paying back of a mortgage. Where we live there are plans to build 6,000 new apartments in the next two years. Assuming these might be bought by people who hope to rent them out during the holiday season this is a huge amount of property to fill with clients. This number of apartments would need over 150,000 rental weeks if the properties were to be let for 26 weeks every year. It is fair to say that if you want to make part of your business in Spain an income from rental properties it would be much more sensible to buy property where a proven track record already exists for return visitors. In other words do not buy new property.

There is also the potential problem that holiday rentals are more lucrative near the coast. When we first moved to Spain we had a rental property, rented out through a major UK company. Our weekly rate was very reasonable and we did receive a lot of business but when I compared bookings of our property (on the coast) to other properties (inland) we had far more bookings.

It is also fair to say that the rental market is also dependent on the choices facing people going on holiday. As I complete this book in 2004 the market seems to be in freefall – since the US is a much more attractive holiday destination as a result of the weak dollar. In 2003 we rented out for 26 weeks. This year, by the end of March, the same apartment had only one confirmed booking – for a week in August!

Nursing homes

There is a long-term business opportunity in Spain for entrepreneurs to set up nursing homes that will be able to accommodate the expat population when they grow older. Many older expats actually sell up and reluctantly return to the cold of the UK. If the right place existed they might be more keen to sell up and move into residential accommodation on the Costa del Sol. After all, as EU pensioners, they qualify for state healthcare so they do not need to go back to the UK to get medical treatment (they will probably have better healthcare in Spain). In fact, recent UK Government publicity suggested that if UK citizens had lived outside the UK for a number of years they might no longer qualify for NHS treatment. For anyone with a medical or nursing qualification and sufficient access to the necessary funding this could be a very good longer-term proposition.

Shops and boutiques

If you sell the right product in the right area there is no question that a small boutique-style shop can be very successful. It helps if you are the only shop offering that product in the immediate vicinity.

The flower shop

We know of one very successful English-style flower shop close to where we live which is not only successful as a retail business from the premises, but the proprietor also has a lot of business providing floral arrangements for some of the well heeled residents in the surrounding area. She is able to run the shop on her own. She has no staff to worry about and her working hours are reasonable. More importantly she has no competitors in the immediate area and any new competitor would need to be very good to take her business. Another example of the need to do your own thorough market research

An art gallery

Others might think that it could be interesting to run an art gallery. Once more a wonderful idea if you can find the right place to operate your business but if you are in the middle of a holiday area where many of the local population are the owners of second homes, which they let out during the height of the season, the market could be very limited. The owners of these properties are unlikely to be major purchasers of art and most of their visitors have not come to the Costa del Sol to buy paintings. Owners are not going to put expensive pictures on the wall only to have then damaged by people renting the property. If you can find the right area for this type of business it could be successful, particularly if you specialise in the work of local artists or if you are an artist yourself and you can sell your own work. Once more, the most important factor is location, location and location.

An English bookshop

English bookshops are another common business venture on the Costa del Sol. They rarely approach the browsing potential of the large bookshops you would expect to find on many high streets in the UK, but they do provide a lifeline for the expatriate who enjoys reading. Most carry a small stock of the latest English best-sellers alongside the tourist guides and usually a good selection of cookery books and gardening books. Where they do score is in their recycling of paperback books. Many offer a service whereby you can 'sell' the books you have read to the bookshop while at the same time you can buy other second-hand books you may not have read. When you have read your purchases you can then recycle them all over again. In essence they operate almost like a paid-for public library.

They are also invaluable as providers of UK-sourced greetings cards and other stationery. I would be surprised if any of the proprietors of these shops were actually getting rich but they do offer a very good service to the expat community and for anyone who loves books it is something worth thinking about.

Interior design

If you have the expertise or a proven track record there are also opportunities here for interior designers. Many properties here do cost a huge amount of money and the buyers of such properties are accustomed to calling in someone to take complete charge of the initial furnishing and decoration. The really wealthy may even ask you back on a regular basis to revamp their home. Once more if you plan to become involved in interior design it could be very useful to have a working knowledge of Spanish so that you can employ and co-ordinate the work of local artisans. If you can do this you will be able to offer a much better service to your clients.

The second-hand furniture shop

This leads me to the final shop which seems to do very well in the coastal area – the second-hand furniture shop. For many people on the coast, redecoration means a complete change of everything, not just the colour of the walls. As a result, many shops have sprung up which resell this unwanted furniture. So long as you have a good eye for quality and are able to negotiate a good price to buy the unwanted goods you should be able to resell it at a reasonable profit to others who want to furnish their new property with good quality, reasonably priced second-hand furniture. Not everyone is rich!

Business and related services

This is a growth area but once more you need to choose your location very carefully. There is no point in opening a secretarial/business service if your chosen area is already well provided for. Choose the area carefully and you could find that there will be a constant demand for fax, photocopying and possibly also Internet/e-mail related services. Not everyone has the appropriate facilities in their own home but in today's electronic-driven world such services are necessary.

Design and printing

If you are also skilled in designing or in using the appropriate computer programmes you should also find a demand for short-run print work – advertising flyers, programmes, menus, invitations and so on. With the new generation of colour printers and colour photocopiers it is not even necessary to have access to a printing press in order to produce very professional-looking documents. Your clients will love what you have created and you will be making a living.

Computer services

Computers are, of course, one key area where there is a real need on the Costa del Sol for expert assistance. Most people now use computers but very few know what to do if problems are experienced. We all need an expert to sort it out. We need someone to help us get our e-mail running smoothly and, if needed, to provide us with new hardware or software which is English-language friendly. Yes, you can buy the hardware or the appropriate programmes in the big electrical stores in Spain but the main language of the new programmes will be Spanish, which may not be a great help to you.

If you are an IT consultant the daily rate will not be as high as that you could charge back in the UK but it could still provide a potentially good income and there is unlikely to be a shortage of work. You may even find that the work simply appears through word of mouth recommendation because your services are vital to many local inhabitants.

If you are an IT expert with additional expertise in the designing and setting up of Web sites you should also find no problem in getting work. More and more people want their own Web site for business reasons and most people at the moment need to employ someone else to set it up and get it onto the Web.

Estate agency and property management

I have never met so many estate agents in my life. So many people here seem to dabble in the buying and selling of property. The high rate of commission is what probably interests the dabblers. With a minimum 5% commission rate and the chance that it will be paid from the 'black' money element of the sale – and therefore paid in cash – it is a very tempting area to get into and so many do.

At the moment there is no legal bar to anyone getting involved but there is always the longer-term possibility that the Spanish regulations will be tightened up and estate agents will require to be licensed. If your long-term career is to be based on this type of work you will need to keep abreast of EU regulations. We have also heard reports that the developers pay even higher rates of commission to those agents who sell the new properties. There is money to be made in real estate on the Costa del Sol at the moment until the rules are tightened up. This is, after all, the equivalent of California in the thirties!!

Another area that is very much in demand due to the large number of second homes on the coast and the large number of holiday lettings is property management. Absentee owners are very keen to appoint key holders who will check their properties on a regular basis for security reasons, organise cleaning and changes of laundry and be on hand to welcome visitors and provide a key collection service.

The basic service is not difficult to organise and, at first sight, appears to be a very easy way to earn an income. After all, charges for the basic service can range from £300 to £500 per year per property. Look after the keys for 20 properties and you could potentially be looking at £10,000 income, which is almost enough to live on here. But it is not easy money. If these 20 properties are all being let successfully you could potentially have 20 turnarounds to organise on a summer Saturday between '10.00 and 16.00 hr'. If the cleaners go sick (which happens) or there are other problems it could be a nightmare. In addition, if there are flight delays the new arrivals may not arrive until after midnight and having paid good money for the rental of the property, they expect to be welcomed and given access. They may also lock themselves out and ring you at two in the morning trying to get back into their apartment. Believe me, we tried this as a potential business opportunity and gave it up. There was just too much aggro.

Cleaning services

Allied to property management there are business opportunities here for individuals who would like to set up a property cleaning business. We know many people locally who are desperate to find good, reliable, honest cleaners to look after their properties in their absence or to prepare them for their arrival.

To run this type of business successfully it could be an advantage to speak Spanish since the most reliable cleaners would be the locals. That is not to say that expats do not make good cleaners but many choose to go back to visit friends in the UK during the height of the summer when it is hot and that is just the time when you, running your new business here, will have the greatest demand for the services of your company. Such a business would not be as lucrative as overall property management since you would only be taking a commission on the hourly earnings of your team of cleaners.

Run in conjunction with a property management business it could be a good way to earn a living but it is not an easy way to be very successful on the Costa del Sol in terms of the financial return.

Painting and decorating

As mentioned earlier there are also many opportunities for the various building trades to find work on the Costa del Sol. We know people who started off with one commission for painting and decorating who accepted it simply because they were bored and wanted something to occupy their minds. The first commission led to more work and before they knew it they were fully employed and actually turning work away.

Hairdressing

Increasingly, new English-run hairdressing salons are opening up on the Costa del Sol and it is an absolutely ideal business to get into. When people go to the hairdresser they like to be able to chat. If they go to a Spanish salon this might be very difficult whereas an English-run salon is perfect – the language for communication is English. There is also the fact that you will have a very large – almost captive – market. There are many women here who are retired, with time on their hands – what better thing to do than to have their hair done once a week, especially since it costs a lot less than it would in most parts of the UK.

The individual salons are becoming more and more sophisticated, offering not just hairdressing but the entire range of beauty treatments which any city centre salon would offer in the UK, albeit at lower prices. The products used are the same as the customer would have been accustomed to since the beauty market is multinational. The brand names are familiar!

It is also interesting that many of these businesses do not follow the established Spanish pattern of closing during the siesta period. This is not an attempt to change the Spanish way of life.

It is a prime example of good, hard-headed business sense since there are potential customers who actually have that siesta time for themselves and it is an excellent opportunity to have their hair done rather than to have a leisurely lunch.

Once more, if you have the right training and background a hairdressing salon could be a very good business opportunity on the Costa del Sol. It might even be an opportunity to have a good business for yourself without actually employing others as staff. If the salon is big enough you could 'rent' a chair to other hairdressers who would officially be self-employed just as you are and who would be responsible for their own tax affairs and social security issues. After all, each person will build up their own group of loyal clients. This is quite common practice in salons in the UK and I am certain that it is moving here.

Language services

If you can get by in Spanish or if you are fluent in the language there are opportunities to teach English as a foreign language. There is a huge demand for English lessons but unless you can communicate easily with the student you could have problems.

If you speak fluent Spanish the world of interpreting and translation is open to you. In fact with the growing number of international conferences which are now held on the Costa del Sol an ability to translate between English and any other European language could be a door-opener to well-paid work. Equally you could offer your services as a translator to the local authorities. Much of their literature is now published in Spanish and in English and they need someone to translate the original into conversational and 'proper' English.

Journalism

If you have a journalistic background, then local English newspapers and magazines could be a source of work. You may not be offered a staff position but they are always looking for articles on a freelance basis and if you contribute often enough, who knows, a full time position might arise.

Gardening

Gardening, both routine and landscape, is much in demand either for private residential work or for the many new developments that are being built. It would be foolish for me to say that you will walk into a major contract to landscape a new development of apartments but if you have the qualifications and a track record and you are good at networking there are possibilities in this area. If you have an impressive portfolio of work done in the UK or qualifications in garden design from some of the internationally recognised UK centres of excellence such as Kew or the Royal Horticultural Society this could open doors for you. The only potential short-term problem could be to learn which plants grow well here and tailor your ideas and designs to this.

There is also a demand for gardeners to look after established gardens. The work is not particularly highly paid since there are many local inhabitants who are already doing this but often they are not really gardeners – they are jobbing handymen – and if someone has invested a lot of time and money on a spectacular garden they might be prepared to pay a little bit more for a gardener who really knows how to look after it and who will make it look even better as the months and years progress. If you have such skills, there is a market for them here.

Satellite television engineers

Many expats have made a good living from satellite television installation. It is not a difficult business to organise but one word of caution needs to be made. Developments built before satellite television was available have been a prime source of business because they do not have a communal receiver. Many of these apartments now have a satellite dish so that potential business has already gone.

Many new developments now have communal satellite receivers and the community bans the installation of private satellite dishes so it is possible that there will be less demand for new installations in the future. There will still be a demand from owners of new villas but the number of villas built compared to the number of apartments is much lower. This may not be a major growth area in the future.

Kennels and catteries

With experience in this area there is a major business opportunity on the Costa del Sol. All you need to do is to find the right premises where you can accommodate the animals and open for business. But one word of caution – just because you have bought a property in the country with land does not give you the right to open the business. Planning permission might restrict the use of the land to agriculture only. Check the restrictions on the land before you buy.

There is not a major tradition among the local population to keep dogs and cats purely as companions but there is a strong tradition in those who come here to live to bring their pets with them. They then have a problem if they want to go back to the UK to visit friends and family – where does the dog or cat go? With the new pet passport scheme they can take their animals back to the UK but this can prove to be very expensive. To fly them back costs a lot. To drive back is equally difficult. It is a two- to three-day drive and on the way the traveller will need to find overnight accommodation which welcomes animals. Many people who live here would welcome good kennel or cattery accommodation for their animals.

This potential business area is not yet totally developed but I believe it has great potential for the future.

Working from home

This is a major business opportunity for anyone from the UK who wants to relocate their family and live on the Costa del Sol. With improvements in communication through mobile phones and e-mail the right business can be run from a distance without the client even knowing that you are living in the sun of the Costa del Sol. ISDN telephone lines are now available in Spain so you can be online 24 hours a day. Mobile phone services are now the equal of anywhere in Europe.

The only negative could be the potential need to visit clients in other parts of the world. If your clients are based in the UK, there would be no problem. There are very good airline connections between Malaga and most major cities in the UK using the major carriers or the so-called low-cost carriers, but should you need to visit clients in other countries, even in Europe, you could have real problems. Most international travel from Malaga would need to be routed through Madrid or Barcelona and this increases the travelling time – time is money. Fares could be very high – in other words, typical European full-price, short-haul fares. When I first lived here I continued to do consultancy work in the industry that I had left. I had a client in Vienna, and a trip from Malaga to Vienna would then have cost me between £1,500 and £2,500 depending on the carrier. This charge would have been included in the bill so, needless to say, my client did not want me to visit Vienna for a meeting.

Having made these criticisms there are many businesses that can be run from a distance, particularly consultancies. If you have expertise that falls into this category you have a real opportunity to live well in the sun.

Business taxation in Spain

All businesses must register for VAT, which in Spain is called *Impuesto sobre el valor anadido* (IVA). This must be charged on all services.

In addition you will be required to pay local business taxes called *Impuesto sobre actividades economicas* (IAE). Just as in the UK, this tax will vary according to location, the type of business and the size of the business. It is collected by the local town hall in the same way as household tax.

You will also be responsible for income tax and payments to the social security system, which as I explained earlier is quite high for the self-employed since you also have to pay the employer's contribution.

Once more this is an area for your *gestor* to get involved in to guide you through the red tape.

Summary

- There is a lot of potential work available on the Costa de Sol.

- It is becoming increasingly easy to identify potential work opportunities which are oriented towards the expat community.

- Spain has a high level of unemployment.

- Consider carefully what you can offer in terms of a service if you choose to be self-employed.

- Do your market research first.

- If you are self-employed and you enter the Spanish social security system you will be responsible for both employee and employer contributions.

- By learning even basic Spanish you will improve your work opportunities.

- Make sure that you are entered into the Spanish social security system by your employer.

- Remember that Spain does follow EU rules with respect to temporary contracts of employment.

- If offered a full time job, ask for a contract of employment.

- Many jobs are available through good networking.

- If you are within easy travelling distance of Gibraltar consider looking for work there.

- If offered work in Gibraltar, ensure that your employer will also cover your family under the Gibraltar social security arrangements.

- Opportunities for running your own business are limited only by your imagination.

13 Social Life

This is one of the more difficult chapters to write and ultimately only you will be able to decide whether the social life you want is what you will find on the Costa del Sol. That is why I say that if you are undecided, you should rent a property first and then make the decision to move here totally if you like the area.

The British way of life

The first point that needs to be made is that on the coast social life can be very British. There is now a very large British community on the Costa del Sol living here on a more or less permanent basis and for many people this is where their social life will exist. For many, their favourite restaurants are English with English food. In many of the coastal areas you will find English pubs – not Spanish bars – and these pubs will often attract their regular clients by typical English attractions such as the weekly pub quiz or football on the large screen television. The beer is on draught and they may even have English brands available. Beer is served in pint mugs imported from the UK and the entire atmosphere is very, very English.

For anyone considering a move in order to pursue a dream of living abroad, I have to be honest and say that the coastal area of the Costa del Sol is not living in real Spain. In many ways it is living in the UK with sun. In our urbanization, which contains 70 apartments, there are only three Spanish families. This picture is repeated in many other urbanizations and some of the larger developments have a complete UK infrastructure with almost every business UK orientated and run.

For many this is a real positive and would be a very strong reason to move here. There is the comfort factor of living in an area where, if you do not want to, you do not even need to even try to learn another language. We know people who have lived here for years who still speak virtually no Spanish. You can benefit from the improved quality of life. You can enjoy the climate. Your children can go to schools where they will be taught in English, possibly even with an English curriculum. Your neighbours will be British. You will become the classic expatriate and your social life will be just that.

Living in real Spain

However, if your personal reason for moving to Spain is to live in real Spain, you will need to move inland. There is virtually nowhere on the coast between Nerja and Tarifa which has not been touched by modern tourism.

If you do decide to move inland you could experience the best of both worlds. When you want a 'fix' of the expatriate lifestyle – an English restaurant or English newspapers – you can jump in the car and drive down to the coast. At other times you will be living in a totally Spanish community and the further you go inland the more unspoilt this community will be. There are still remote villages where, unless you speak, or are prepared to learn Spanish, you may indeed feel very isolated and at a great disadvantage. Some of these villages have hardly changed for centuries.

There will be many local families whose ancestors have lived in the same village for centuries and whose properties have been handed down from generation to generation. The lifestyle in these villages is very different from that on the coast. The goatherds still lead their flocks out to the best local grazing grounds. The transport of goods between one village and the next might still be by donkey or mule. If you happen to buy the local property which has a good well and therefore a good supply of water you might find that one of the locals brings his animals down to your property every day for water since he has been doing that every day throughout his life and may even have a 'right' to do this. Take away this privilege and you will be very unpopular with the local population.

Eating out

It is perhaps the restaurant culture that really differentiates the expatriate and the person who wants to live in the Spanish style. If you want to remain British there is no shortage of restaurants that offer the food you would expect to see on the menu in the old country.

If you want a full English cooked breakfast this is readily available the length of the coast. If you enjoy a traditional English Sunday lunch with roast beef and Yorkshire pudding you will have no problems in finding a suitable restaurant. Chinese, Indian, Italian, Thai, and virtually every other cuisine you might hanker after is available on the coast but there may be very few restaurants which actually serve Spanish food. Go five miles inland and the food will be Spanish with some difficulty in finding an alternative.

As I write this chapter I have just returned from a most wonderful Sunday lunch in a Spanish restaurant ten miles from the coast. My fellow diners were almost totally local residents and there was not an empty table in the entire restaurant. The food was wonderful and very reasonably priced as we discovered when the bill arrived – about the same price as a steak house menu in the UK – but it was a truly Spanish lunch. Salads of various types as a starter some with local sausage included, chorizo, followed by main courses which included wild mountain rabbit, wild boar, lamb chops, local fish, game and a huge selection of other local produce but everything on the menu was cooked in the Spanish style with lots of olive oil, tomatoes, vegetables and herbs and no French fries to be seen on the menu. In this same restaurant the bread was locally produced, freshly baked and still warm from the oven.

I would have to say that many of my fellow residents on the Costa del Sol would not enjoy such a lunch because it was not traditional English and they would be unwilling to try some of the delicious dishes on the menu. This is the difference between living here as someone who wants to experience Spain and someone who wants to live the expatriate life in the sun. There is a place for both but you, the reader, must decide what you want in your life.

Special events

Despite the fact that Spain and the UK are both part of Europe there are major differences in the way special events are celebrated.

Christmas

Christmas Day is a major event in the UK but the Spanish really celebrate Christmas on the 6th January, the Feast of the Three Kings (*Dia de Reyes*). This is when Spanish children receive their presents. This is when the major processions take place in the streets and they can be spectacular processions! This part of Christmas is the major part of the holiday but to the British this is the end of the Christmas period and for most Brits the holiday is over. Some adjustment is therefore required.

Speaking to many new arrivals on the coast they are often taken by surprise that in a very Catholic country, Christmas does not appear to produce the hustle and bustle that you would expect in the UK around the Christmas season. There is not the same frenzied shopping. The supermarkets are not full of people stocking up as if there was going to be a siege. There are no carol singers and while even the smallest towns have their lights in the streets and squares there is a noticeable absence of domestic Christmas trees especially in Spanish areas. The Spanish do not decorate their houses the way we would do and there are far fewer January sales.

Easter

Holy week is also a major part of the calendar on the Costa del Sol with many towns and cities almost brought to a halt by the celebrations. Although it is a little bit far away from the coast proper, Seville has the most amazing celebrations for Holy Week, *Semana Santa*, and the city basically closes down for a week. It is such a large festival that it can be almost impossible to book a hotel room in the city.

San Juan

Summer festivities around the Feast of San Juan are another major part of the calendar here and most towns, even the smallest, have the most amazing and elaborate festivities and firework displays to celebrate the summer solstice.

There appear to be far more public holidays in Spain generally and the first thing that any new arrival here needs to do is to buy a Spanish calendar. Only by doing this will you be able to anticipate when all the shops and services will be closed and in the process you will save yourself a great deal of irritation and inconvenience when you discover that there is nowhere to buy the food to put on your table because you did not know that there was a public holiday. In our first year here we were occasionally very frustrated by public holidays. I have provided a list of the public holidays on the Costa del Sol in Appendix 3.

Adjustment to time differences

When it comes to mealtimes the British eat early and the Spanish eat late. This can be a positive when it comes to getting a table in a restaurant. It is very noticeable, particularly in the height of the holiday season where we live, that in the early evening the chatter in local restaurants is almost totally in English whereas after 22.00 the conversations are almost totally in Spanish and the Spanish families might sit in the restaurant until one in the morning. There are often negative comments made about the noise that the local population makes. This is not really true. It is just that the Spanish population operate on a different time clock and when the British population are thinking about going to bed the Spanish are just waking up.

This does need to be taken into consideration if you choose to live in an area that is oriented towards the holiday market since a large number of Spanish do holiday on the Costa del Sol in August and restaurants can be quite noisy until the early hours of the morning.

Similarly Sunday lunch will start for the Brits at 12.30 or 13.00 and be over by 16.00 whereas the Spanish will only arrive for lunch at 15.00 and lunch can last until 20.00.

Another irritation can be the time difference of one hour between the UK and Spain. This can be a problem if some of the

TV programmes you like to watch are shown late at night. As a result you often find yourself sitting up until 1 am.

Summary

- Think carefully about the type of social life you want to have on the Costa del Sol.

- If you want to live the expatriate lifestyle and speak English all the time – live on the coast.

- If you want to live abroad – buy inland.

14 Leisure, Sports and Keeping in Touch

The climate of the Costa del Sol lends itself to a wonderful life outdoors and there is no shortage of leisure and sports facilities for all age groups.

Golf

Many of the signs along the motorways and the main roads proclaim the Costa del Sol to be the Costa del Golf and this is not an overexaggeration by any means. Between Tarifa and Malaga there are around 25 golf courses with the majority to be found between Sotogrande and Marbella, with more planned. Some, such as Valderrama are world class, championship courses which are often used for major international events and many have been designed by professional golfers like Sevi Ballesteros. The green fees cover all price ranges but to play on some courses will involve a very high cost indeed.

> You could find yourself paying more than £100 for a game of golf.

The climate is of course ideal for golf. The only months of the year when it might be impossible to play are in July and August when temperatures in the middle of the day are just too hot to be on the golf course and the sun is too strong. At other times of the year apart from the few days when the rain is torrential the courses are ideal. The courses are impeccably maintained and some have the most spectacular views of the coast and of North Africa.

If you are a keen golfer it could be a very positive move to buy in an urbanization that offers residents reduced fees on membership of the golf course which is part of the development. In this way you can have your ideal property and your golf all as part of the same package and there will also be the social benefits of belonging to that particular course.

For keen golfers who can afford the green fees the Costa del Sol is a paradise. A list of golf courses is included in Appendix 7.

Tennis

There are municipal tennis courts the length of the coast and many urbanizations that include golf courses also have tennis courts but I have to say that I was surprised that there are not more tennis courts here when the climate is considered. It may be due to the fact that up until the last few years the average age of the person who relocated to the coast was older than the average age of the keen tennis player. This situation could change in the future.

Sailing and water sports

There is no shortage of marinas between Malaga and Tarifa. They range from the super exclusive such as Puerto Banus to the more affordable. Whichever marina you choose to visit you will find boats of all sizes for charter, either sailing or powered, and you will find boat owners who offer deep-sea fishing or dolphin watching. All you need to do is to get into your car, explore the marinas and make your choice. The Mediterranean is a key part of life here and it is used extensively as a resource. If you own a boat you do need to shop around and find which marina offers the best mooring facilities at the best possible price.

If you are a windsurfer, Tarifa is often called the European windsurfing capital.

Hiking, climbing and walking

The Costa del Sol is a paradise for lovers of the great outdoors. There are a number of national parks within easy reach of the coast and if you live inland you might even live right on the edge of one.

Among these national parks is the Sierra de las Nieves national park, which is just inland from Marbella. Further afield you will find the Sierra Nevada, the highest mountain range in Europe after the Alps. Apart from wonderful areas for walking and hiking, you will also find rock climbing opportunities if you are more energetic (or younger!). If all you want to do is to put on a stout pair of walking shoes and ramble through the hills the ideal area is Las Alpujarras, the range of mountains and hills between the Sierra Nevada and Malaga. Here you will find some of the remotest villages in Europe, perched high in the hills and virtually unchanged for centuries. This area is becoming a bit more visited (and developed) thanks to books such as *Driving over Lemons*, which was a major literary success a few years ago.

Wherever you choose to go walking, the countryside behind the coast will astound you. Within a few miles of the coastal strip you really do enter a different and totally unspoilt world. It is blissfully quiet. There are no cranes to be seen anywhere. You can get away from your fellow man and all you will see is the occasional rabbit scampering ahead of you, startled by your presence, and the buzzards, kestrels and even eagles soaring overhead on the air currents.

This is an area which so many of the summer visitors to the Costa del Sol never see – they do not bother to go inland – but this area really should not be missed if you enjoy nature. It is one of the last unspoilt regions of Western Europe and it is by no stretch of the imagination inaccessible.

Birds and insects

If you are into bird watching in a big way, the area around Gibraltar is probably the best place in Europe to see those birds you have always wanted to catch a glimpse of. Here you are literally 12 miles from Africa and many migratory birds stop off here before their final flight to the warmth of the African winter. If bird life really interests you, then you need to buy the appropriate books. You may even want to venture slightly further afield to the Cota Donana in Cadiz province where bird watching holidays are organised in the National Park.

While talking about wildlife it is worth mentioning at this point that overall on the Costa del Sol there is not too much to worry those with phobias. Insect life is not as bad as it is on other parts of the Mediterranean coast. Yes, you will find spiders but they are not huge although there are a few species which can give quite a nasty bite if disturbed. There is a surprising lack of moths in the evening. If your phobia is beetles they can be found and in some of the older established areas there may be cockroaches but there is not a real problem.

There are snakes but apparently there are no venomous snakes in Spain.

The surprising sports

Considering the fact that you are so close to Africa and the climate is very hot in the summer and very mild in the winter this is probably one of the few regions in Europe where you can water-ski in the morning and ski on snow in the afternoon.

There is a very well developed skiing area in the Sierra Nevada, behind Malaga, which many of the local population use throughout the winter months. Generally, the snow cover is very good although it can be a bit later in the season before it becomes really good. You will find all the facilities you would expect in the Alps, Switzerland or Austria but at a fraction of the price and you will have a wonderful winter sports holiday without having to travel very far from your new location.

The proximity of the mountain ranges also means that some of the more adventurous sports like hang-gliding and parascending are also available

Social clubs

If you move here and you want to organise your life around social clubs you will find no shortage of opportunities. The only problem might be choosing the club.

Your decision when you move to the Costa del Sol might depend on your interests when you lived in the UK. Just going through one of the local English language newspapers for the coast I can list the following possibilities.

- Should you want to belong to the Royal British Legion (Spanish branches) there are opportunities in Estepona, Mijas, Fuengirola, Benalmadena, Nerja or Torremolinos.

- Conservatives Abroad are represented in Fuengirola and Mijas – there is also a Costa del Sol International Labour Group which operates in Fuengirola, Nerja, Torremolinos and Estepona.

- The Rotary Club is present in Benalmadena, Benahavis, Estepona, Fuengirola, Marbella and San Pedro.

- The Toastmasters' Club is contactable in several areas on the coast.

These are the clubs that have international recognition, but there are many others which would welcome English-speaking expatriates. Some of these clubs offer services to very specialised sections of the community, some are more wide-ranging but you do need to look at the possibilities when you move here and decide which, if any, you wish to join. The contact numbers are in all the local English language newspapers. Most offer very good social possibilities and the opportunity to meet others who have taken the same decision.

Religion

If you are planning a move to the Costa del Sol and your religion is very important to you this could have a major effect on where you might choose to live. Spain is still a very Catholic country so wherever you live there will be a Catholic Church which you can attend so long as you speak Spanish, but if you are not Catholic and you wish to play a part in the church life of your chosen faith you need to choose your location more carefully.

- The Church of England is represented in Malaga, Nerja, Competa, Fuengirola, Calahonda, Coin, San Pedro, Sotogrande, Estepona and obviously in Gibraltar.

- If you are Muslim there are mosques in Marbella, Fuengirola and Malaga.

- Methodist is restricted to Gibraltar and Sotogrande.

- Jehovah's Witnesses have access to their faith in Torremolinos, Fuengirola, Malaga, San Pedro, and Torre del Mar.

- Baptists have churches available in Los Boliches, Torremolinos, Nerja, Fuengirola, Calahonda, Marbella, La Linea, Mijas, Gibraltar and Benalmedena.

- Presbyterians (the way I was brought up) are not too well catered for. There are churches in Fuengirola and Gibraltar. Perhaps not too many Presbyterians live here!!

- The Mormon faith is catered for in Fuengirola, Malaga, La Linea, Algeciras and Gibraltar.

So religion is well catered for on the Costa del Sol.

Charity work

There are many charities operating on the Costa del Sol. Among the highest profile charities are Cudeca, which does wonderful work for cancer sufferers. There are also a number of animal charities such as Adana which looks after homeless dogs and cats. Many of these charities are run by British expatriates. After all, charity work has been a mainstay of British social life for generations.

The charitable organisations here are always looking for new blood and if you really want to be involved and have the time to do it, you could find charity work to be a very rewarding interest in your new life. Like everything, there are positives and negatives. Involvement will provide you with new social contacts with those who already work for the charity – the positive. Unfortunately many of these charities are run as social groups primarily and charities as a secondary function and new members in the group can be frowned upon because they want to introduce changes and those changes may not be welcomed by the old guard – this can be a negative.

Communication

Newspapers, magazines and books

If you are planning to relocate to Spain and your daily fix of an English newspaper is important, you will have no problems whatsoever. Modern technology has resulted in the fact that all the popular UK newspapers are now published in Spain and are available from the newsagent first thing in the morning. Whatever paper you buy it will be identical to the one you would buy in the UK apart from a few adverts, which are local to Spain, and the weather forecast which shows the Iberian peninsula rather than the British Isles. The paper is obviously sent electronically to the Spanish publisher every day. The only negative is that your daily newspaper will cost considerably more than it would back in the UK and the Sunday papers do not have all the supplements (or the free CDs or DVDs).

There are also many English language newspapers and magazines produced locally. The main newspapers are *Sur* in English and the *Town Crier*, both published weekly on the Costa del Sol. Added to these are the magazines printed on a monthly or quarterly basis in many of the towns along the coast. Some of these are very glossy indeed and they are all free since their existence depends on the many businesses who buy advertising in their pages because they want to sell to the expatriate community.

Books are another matter. If you are an avid reader you could find the Costa del Sol frustrating. There is an English language section in the book departments of the major department store, El Corte Ingles, but it is not as extensive as you might wish. For the most part it will stock the titles that are currently best-sellers in the UK but it may not provide you with the opportunity to simply browse with a view to buying. There are also many English bookshops along the coast. They are very good and often have a good selection but once more the simple laws of business dictate that they basically stock the few titles which are currently best-sellers or they offer a very good selection of guide books, recipe books and tourist oriented titles. Where they can be very useful is that many do buy unwanted paperbacks and resell them.

Ultimately if you are an avid reader it would be better to have a computer and buy your books online from suppliers such as Amazon. We use them all the time and deliveries are usually within a week but it is not quite the same as browsing in a bookshop.

There are more limited selections of English language books available in branches of El Corte Ingles or FNAC.

Television

This is the one area in which communication has changed dramatically over the last few years. Television and radio today is almost totally digital and armed with the appropriate satellite receiving dish you can live here and enjoy all the programmes you might want to view or the radio stations you want to listen to no matter which country you originally come from. All you need is the appropriate viewing card to decode the signal. The various companies who supply viewing cards cannot supply them to a Spanish address but they can to a UK address. So you should maintain an official address in the UK until such time that the EU laws change to accommodate this new technology and allow free access to viewing cards whatever your address.

Radio

There are English language radio stations that broadcast on the coast but if you have a satellite dish you will also have access to all the UK radio stations.

Where I do have to ring warning bells is to advise anyone who comes to live here not to be ripped off by fellow Brits who run satellite installation services and who will install a satellite dish and charge you hundreds of pounds to provide a viewing card. So long as you have an address in the UK the appropriate card can be sent to that address – it may even be a free to view card – and if plugged into your decoder in Spain it should work perfectly at the moment. In fact now that many British television stations have been switched onto the Astra satellite, even a viewing card is not necessary – your satellite dish will pick up the signal. You should also avoid buying a card for your decoder locally. It could cost you a lot of money for something which is available to your UK address for very little and the chances are that the card is pirated anyway.

The other point which needs to be made is that in some new developments there will be television points in the main rooms but these will only be capable of receiving the stations which the urbanization has agreed to provide to its residents. There may be a total ban on the installation of your own, private satellite dish which would allow you to receive the stations you want to either watch or listen to should you have the appropriate viewing card. If you are buying new and television is important to you in your new life you must investigate what stations you might be able to receive. Ask the questions before you buy the property.

The whole question of satellite television reception is one which needs to be clarified by the various national authorities in the future. For the moment if you live here, satellite television is a reality. Continued access to the stations you watched back home is possible. It need not cost you a fortune but be careful about those who try to charge you a large amount of money for something you could have for a lot less or indeed something which might cost you nothing each month. Your only cost would then be the initial installation of the dish.

Telephone and mail

In this area you will be totally dependent on the services provided by your Spanish hosts on the Costa del Sol.

Telephone

The Spanish national telephone system, Telefonica, is excellent (most of the time). The actual service provided is the equal of if not better than the similar service provided by BT in the UK although there can be individual line problems. We were surprised by the fact that our normal telephone line in Spain has an automatic telephone answering service, which allowed us to reprogramme the message to incoming callers into an

English language message. On the Costa del Sol you do not need a telephone answering machine. When there is a problem and that is infrequent, there is no problem in ringing Telefonica in order to speak to an English language operator.

There are also a number of telephone service providers who offer cheap rate calls between Spain and the rest of the world. These companies are worth contacting since they could save you money when you call your friends and family but it is not my place in this book to provide advertising material for them. Suffice to say, they exist and they are not difficult to find once you live here.

Spanish mobile services are excellent and offer all the facilities you might have expected in the UK whether you choose a monthly contract or a pay-as-you-go telephone. The one point worth repeating here is that it is not difficult to get a replacement chip for your existing phone in order to switch to the Spanish system. You do not need to buy a new telephone.

The postal system

The postal system is a different matter. In the UK, we have been spoiled by a world-class postal delivery service, which despite problems in recent years is still the service by which the rest of the world judges postal services.

This is not the case in Spain. The local post offices are geared to the official local population and where we live the queues in the post office can be very irritating – particularly in the lead up to Christmas. Letters are delivered to your home if you live in town but if you live in an area which is classified as being in the country the letters will only be delivered to one collection point and you then have to collect your mail from this point. There may not even be a collection point in which case you will need to have a post box address although these can be difficult to organise and in some areas there is a long waiting list. There is very little security at these communal collection points and therefore you can have the constant worry that someone may intercept your mail. If you know that mail is expected you look carefully for each delivery. If you do not expect mail you will never know whether it was delivered or not.

My answer to this has been very simple. I use e-mail whenever possible. In doing this I bypass the services of the post office and I know instantly whether or not my message has been received. I would encourage anyone who relocates here to have a computer and to use e-mail as their preferred means of communication.

Computers

There are very few of us who could survive in the modern world without computers. They provide access to our friends and to the outside world. They provide access to the Internet. When you live in Spain you really do need to have a computer that still talks in your language – a UK computer. The software will be in English. Access to the Internet will be in English and in real terms it will be no different from accessing your e-mail or going on the Internet in the UK – such is the wonder of modern communication. However, if you buy a computer here the software will almost certainly be in Spanish. The keyboard will be slightly different because Spanish is a language with accents over some letters and this has to be accommodated on the keyboard. You might have problems.

Therefore, when it comes to computer services, you need to find a computer expert locally who sorts out your problems, provides new software and organises e-mail or Internet access in English. Find the right person and you will have no problems in contact with the outside world in the long term. This person will be your lifeline on occasions.

Power surges and power cuts

One point that should be made about using computers and other electrical equipment in Spain is the possibility of surges in the power supply, which could damage the equipment. Special surge protecting plugs can be bought and you should protect your computer equipment by buying one.

The other irritation with respect to your PC is the possibility of power cuts which happen much more frequently than in the UK. When working on important documents you should either set up automatic save every few minutes or save your document manually on a very regular basis. I learned this the hard way when a whole day's work disappeared as a result of a ten second power cut.

Summary

In deciding where you want to live choose your location according to your leisure interests and the clubs you might want to join.

• Charity work can also be a valuable contribution to your social life.

- If you are an avid reader be prepared to order your books online from an Internet store.

- If computers are important to your life bring one with you from the UK with UK programmes and find where your nearest computer expert has a business to deal with problems.

- If possible use e-mail as a means of communication rather than letters.

15 Pets

Many British people considering the move to Spain will want to take their pets with them. Since the relaxation of the quarantine laws a few years ago by the UK this is no longer a problem and even if you plan to make the occasional trip back to the old country your beloved dog or cat can be a part of your new life here. Properly vaccinated, microchipped and with the correct paperwork, the 'pet passport', your pets can travel with you.

Importing your dog or cat

To import dogs or cats into Spain they must be microchipped so that they are identified as domestic animals and apart from the vaccinations that they need to have in the UK they also need an additional vaccination against rabies. This potentially fatal disease is not something you actually need to worry about in Spain since there has been no human case in Spain or Portugal for a very long time. You may, however, wish to transport your animals through France where rabies is endemic in the wild fox population and that is why rabies vaccination is mandatory. If you take your animals back to the UK they will need rabies vaccination and a certificate showing that they have antibodies in their blood. All this is part of the 'pet passport' system.

The other normal vaccinations for dogs are leptospirosis, parvovirus, hepatitis, distemper and kennel cough while cats should be vaccinated against feline gastro-enteritis and typhus.

Leishmaniasis

The real worry for dog owners in Spain is a disease called leishmaniasis, which is transmitted by sand flies. Many wild or rescued dogs in Spain unfortunately are infected by this nasty parasite. Your Spanish vet can organise a simple blood test to find out if your dog has been infected and, if treated early, the disease can be controlled very well by drugs and the dog can lead a normal life. Untreated, the parasite causes a disease which to the layman is a cross between malaria and AIDS and it can be fatal. There is a serious effect to the dog's immune system, which can leave it open to other infections, or it can cause problems with the dog's coat through skin disease. It is not normally transmitted from the dog to humans so you do not have to worry on this count.

Other precautions

The one thing you absolutely have to ensure in Spain, particularly with dogs is that they wear a protective anti-flea and anti-tick collar at all times since this will protect against many of the potential diseases which are transmitted by biting insects and ticks. In country areas you also need to be careful about potential poisoning of your animals since it is still fairly common practice for farmers to lay down poisoned food to control foxes and rats. If you are a dog lover you will know only too well how good dogs are at finding illicit food that they are determined to eat. Be careful!

Dangerous dogs

Recently a dog registration scheme has been introduced on the Costa del Sol that requires all dogs to be microchipped, and some breeds should be registered with the authorities. These tend to be the larger breeds and your Spanish vet can advise you whether your family pet falls into the 'dangerous' category. I have to say that some of the breeds which are on the 'dangerous' list would not be my idea of a dangerous dog but that is the law.

Among the commonly recognised 'dangerous' breeds (including crosses) are Pit Bull and all Bull breeds, Rottweilers, Akitas, German Shepherds, but even Labradors in theory could be included! The law is based on size and weight – all dogs over 20 kilos. Even if your dog does not officially belong to one of these breeds but it has a history of biting someone in the past it could be classified as dangerous. Dogs falling into this category should be microchipped, registered with the local town hall and should have a certificate from the police (the *Guardia Civil*). They should be muzzled in public areas and always kept on a very short lead. The fences around your property should also by law be two metres high if you own a 'dangerous' dog.

The law also states that a resident of Spain who owns one of these dangerous dogs may have to undergo psychological tests. You may even be asked to demonstrate that you can control your dog. Do check out this new law with your vet who should be able to advise you and help you complete any forms.

In practice on the Costa del Sol this law, which was only introduced in 2000, is not yet strictly enforced in every municipality on the Costa del Sol – but it does exist. You also need to realise that any damage to property or people caused by unsupervised dogs will be your responsibility under the law therefore you should take out insurance to cover any third-party claims.

Other restrictions

Legally, dogs are also prohibited from many beaches and some urbanizations do not allow the owners of property to keep pets. We have heard conflicting information on this potential rule – note that it is a rule of the urbanization and not the law of Spain – and if challenged the dog owner might actually win the right to keep their animal but when you first arrive in a new country you do not really want to get involved in this type of problem so check first and you may avoid a lot of heartache.

Veterinary care

Veterinary care on the Costa del Sol is very good and surprisingly inexpensive compared to the fees we used to pay in SW London but it is very notable that many of the vets on the coast are not Spanish. They are British, German and Dutch. These are the vets who, back in the UK, I would have referred to as vets who specialise in small animals – in other words, pets. There are Spanish vets but they are more involved with looking after the commercial animals, the farm animals, because the one thing you learn here very quickly is that the local population do not keep pet animals to any great extent.

The local attitude to dogs and cats

This is one thing that can upset the new arrival on the Costa del Sol. In Spain, dogs are not always kept as pets.

They are generally kept for hunting and you often see cars with a trailer full of dogs going off into the countryside. These dogs have to work and if they do not produce the desired hunting success they may simply end up being thrown out and left to live in the country – *campo* dogs.

Nowhere have I seen so many apparently abandoned dogs. It breaks my heart sometimes to see beautiful dogs foraging for food in the *campo* (the countryside). The local animal charity where we live has a wonderful rescue centre in the hills behind the coast, which is basically supported by the expat community, and if you go to this rescue as an animal lover you will want to take all the dogs home but that is just not possible.

It is also an unfortunate fact of life here that many of the abandoned dogs and cats are in that situation because they were owned by expat families who did not live here 12 months of the year and when they returned to their northern European home they simply threw their 'pet' dog or cat out on the motorway on the return journey to Malaga airport.

Cats as pets do not seem to be terribly popular with the local population but there are many feral or semi-feral cats all over the coast. I find it so sad that when you go near some of the restaurant areas to see colonies of cats who manage to keep themselves alive by raiding the rubbish bins. Some of them are so beautiful but they are basically wild. There are many individuals here who try to round them up and take them to sympathetic vets who will neuter them for a very small fee so that they stop breeding.

If, like us, you are animal lovers, you may be very tempted to give a home to many of these abandoned animals. Unfortunately this may not be possible unless you have huge amounts of land and an unlimited budget but we do have many friends who now have five or more dogs, all rescued from the *campo*. At least they are playing a part in looking after some of these unwanted animals.

Transporting your animals

When you first come to Spain with your pets the decision on how you bring them here is entirely up to you. If you have the correct documentation you can either travel by car through France and

Spain – potentially a three day drive – but remember you will have to find pet-friendly accommodation on the journey or you can fly the animals to Spain. Also if you transport dogs or cats through France they must be vaccinated against rabies at least one month before transportation. Accompanied animals arriving with their owner by air may be imported into Spain without rabies vaccination.

From a personal viewpoint I consider that a long car journey could potentially be more distressing for the animal when compared to a relatively short flight. Airlines licensed to carry animals look after them very well indeed. They travel in a properly designed box in a heated part of the aircraft hold. They are not loaded onto the plane until the very last minute and they are first off the plane on arrival in Spain. Should you wish someone else to make the necessary arrangements for travel there are many companies in the UK who can do this. They will attend to all the paperwork and liaise with similar companies at the Spanish end of the chain who will collect your pets from the airport and even deliver them to your new address.

There are also companies who offer road transport of your valuable pets with stopovers at dog-friendly hotels.

One point worth considering at the time of your removal from the UK to the Costa del Sol is to ask the transporting company to collect your precious pets and keep them in their kennels or cattery during the period when your possessions are actually being packed. This avoids the animal experiencing the potential distress of the actual packing process. You can then set the exact date when your pet is delivered to your new address.

Summary

- Relaxation of quarantine regulations has made it easier to transport pets to and from Spain.

- Be very aware of leishmaniasis in dogs.

- Ensure that your pets wear flea and tick collars.

- Check whether your dog is classified as 'dangerous' under Spanish law.

- Veterinary care is excellent.

- Consider carefully the best way to transport your pets.

16 Is a Move to the Costa del Sol Right for You? – A Summary

Only you and your family can make this decision and only after considerable research. Do not rush into a decision.

The preceding pages will provide you with a lot of information about life on the Costa del Sol, both positive and negative. I have tried to be honest and objective about all aspects. Living here is not living in the UK and in many respects it also differs from life in other parts of Spain. There is now a huge expatriate community, which can make life easier, particularly if you do not speak fluent Spanish. However this also results in the fact that in many ways it is not really living abroad. One local friend actually commented that when the British lost their empire they started to colonise the Costa del Sol!

Climate

The climate is absolutely wonderful and it makes such a difference to life to have sun for so much of the year but if you find the summer heat too much to bear, you could have problems. To deal with this you need to choose your property very carefully. You also need to appreciate that it can be much cooler and very wet indeed in the winter.

Pace of life

The pace of life is wonderfully relaxed and many people reckon that a move to the Costa del Sol will add years to your life expectancy. Short term the relaxed pace of life can cause real problems. Siesta and the 'mañana' culture can really irritate. If you have been accustomed to a society in which things happen at the time arranged for your appointment you might have very real frustrations when you first move to the Costa del Sol. When you realise that things will happen, sometime, you learn to accept this and the stress disappears.

Property

The choice of property is another potential minefield. There is a huge choice of available property. This in itself can be a problem. You might see so many properties it becomes almost impossible to make a decision. There is also a huge geographical area to choose from either on the coast or inland so, if in doubt, rent first.

There is an almost unbelievable amount of building going on the entire length of the coast and you really need to look carefully and consider what could be built around your dream property. You could suddenly find your dream turning into a nightmare – your wonderful view could disappear totally.

Be very careful also about buying new property off-plan. It can appear to be very attractive in terms of the prices offered but once more problems can occur. We know of individuals who have experienced nightmare scenarios after moving into newly built property – plumbing not properly installed, sewage bubbling up through the ground and life on a continuing building site for months (or even years).

Similarly the idyllic property in the country can turn into a private hell if you are at the end of a dirt track that suddenly turns into thick mud as soon as it rains.

Position

To be really happy in the long term you also need to consider very carefully what you want or expect in life. The Costa del Sol is still a holiday destination so this means that during the height of the summer, many areas can be very busy. The roads are busy. The restaurants and bars are full and life can go on until very late in the night. If you choose a holiday area you must recognise this. That wonderful quiet apartment or townhouse may turn into a very noisy place to live for a few weeks in the summer or during half-term holidays. On the other hand that same area can be dead during the low season. Many of the properties around you may be locked and shuttered and you may have no neighbours. Life could be lonely but perhaps you want and enjoy solitude. We certainly prefer the low season.

> Whatever you buy, you do need to use a good local lawyer who will look after your interests. Your lawyer needs to check that all debts on the property have been paid since they will follow the property. If not and you experience problems your new life on the coast could soon turn into something you regret and it may not be easy to get out of it.

Living legally

Living legally in Spain is also an important consideration in your new life. The rules as set out in both Spanish and European law are simple but it has to be said that there are many people living here who do interpret the rules very liberally. That is their choice and the chances are that they will be able to live in this way for a very long time without any problems. However the Spanish authorities may decide to tighten up on some of the rules and unless you are prepared for this, once again, you could have problems.

Tax

With respect to your potential tax situation in Spain you should discuss this with your *gestor* when you have found one locally. Spain is not the tax haven it once was and the authorities, local and national, are tightening up on taxation. Taxes are at the moment lower than they are in many other EU states but despite this the black economy continues to be very common but at some stage the authorities here may realise that a stronger clampdown on tax evasion could bring a lot more income to the government. According to some commentators in the Spanish press the burden of taxation on those who pay their taxes could be reduced considerably.

Shopping

If you are a shopaholic the Costa del Sol could lose its appeal after a few months or years. The shops in many of the tourist areas are very tourist-oriented and may not offer you the type of selection you prefer. There are now more and more shopping malls appearing and if this form of shopping is the one that appeals to you, you will be in heaven. Many have branches of high street names you will recognise.

Shopping for the everyday necessities of life is not a problem and the cost of living on a day-to-day basis is very inexpensive indeed. The quality of the local produce is excellent and vegetables or fruit in season is sold almost at a giveaway price. Household goods are less expensive than they are in the UK and white goods are certainly cheaper. Insurance – whether for your house and possessions or for your car – is much cheaper than in most parts of the UK. Overall the cost of running a car is much lower since petrol and diesel are much cheaper.

The arts

If you are one of those individuals for whom theatre, cinema or the other performing arts are of vital importance, the Costa del Sol is a bit of a desert. There are cinemas but they are not as common as they are in other countries (or indeed other parts of Spain) and the films may not be shown in English. You may have to drive for half an hour to get to your nearest cinema.

Theatre is virtually non-existent. It exists but not to the extent you would find in the UK. There are no touring groups taking the most recent London West End hits out to the provinces. Where it does exist it is unlikely that you will see any big names appearing on stage here. There is theatre in the big cities but plays will be performed in Spanish and once more if you do not understand the language you are at a real disadvantage. Opera and ballet performances are very few and far between. Cities like Malaga have a good selection of museums and art galleries but once you have seen the exhibitions there might be nothing new to see for a long time. Other smaller towns may have a local museum but they can be visited very quickly and you will probably only want to visit once.

With respect to the arts the Costa del Sol is lacking. We have friends who have to return to London every few months to gorge themselves on theatre and the performing arts. Indeed many of the Spanish population feel the same and they have to travel to Seville or Madrid to enjoy theatre and concerts.

Education

Education for your children is good but you need to decide whether you prefer (and can afford) private education or whether you are happy for your children to attend Spanish state schools. The latter have benefits when it comes to language skills being developed but as I said in the education chapter it can pose problems during teenage years when children are at their most difficult in terms of building relationships or being unkind to their peers. Unhappy children are not conducive to a happy new life in the sun for the parents.

Healthcare

Healthcare is amazingly good on the Costa del Sol. Emergency treatment is second to none and can be depended on totally. The cost of private health insurance is very low. If you can afford private healthcare the quality of GP care is excellent and should you need to go into hospital, the majority of hospitals are much better than their equivalent NHS hospital. The only negative could be the public sector if you are dependent on this. The waiting times in the GP surgery are similar to those you have already experienced and until you have total command of Spanish, you might find it more difficult to find an English-speaking doctor.

Leisure and social activities

Leisure and sports facilities are excellent. Remember this is a holiday area and visitors expect good facilities. If you are a golfer you will be in heaven (if you can afford the green fees) but most other sports are also available. If you simply enjoy the big outdoors there are very few places in Europe with such a wide variety of outdoor pursuits. Hill walking, rock climbing, and even winter sports are all available on the Costa del Sol.

Social life is excellent but it falls into two distinct areas. You can either build your circle of friends within the expatriate community, which is very easy, or you can try to break out into the local community, which is a little bit more difficult. Once more, without some ability to speak Spanish you might find your social life remains the expatriate variety.

There are restaurants to cater for all food tastes and eating out is very inexpensive compared to other European countries. The only problem on the coast can be to find typical Spanish restaurants but you only have to go a few miles inland to do this. There you will find wonderful Spanish restaurants where you will eat very well indeed for not very much money.

Communication

Communication is good. The telephone system is well developed. You have satellite television with a choice of English-speaking channels and most English newspapers can be bought locally, having been printed in Spain, on the day of publication. There are many companies who now offer reasonably priced Internet access and the increasing number of specialist computer engineers and consultants can take care of your IT needs.

Work

If you move here without an immediate source of income, there is work but it may not fall into your lap on the first day you arrive or start to look for work. So much of the work that might be available can still come from networking or from people you know.

Setting up a business takes time and once more the work may not arrive on the day you open the doors of your new business. Potential clients need to know that the business exists. If you take a job working for someone else you need to be careful and ensure that you have a contract of employment or you need to accept that you might have a job today and none tomorrow. If you set up your own business you need to be prepared for the fact that social security payments on a self-employment basis are a lot higher than you might expect. If you can afford to look after yourself and your family without recourse to any potential need for benefits or Spanish state healthcare you do not really have a problem but if you do, be careful.

If your business involves a lot of travelling to parts of Europe other than the UK you also need to take note. Travel from Malaga to the rest of Europe can be very expensive and it is the clients who will indirectly have to pay for your travel. This could make the difference between being able to offer a very good service at a daily rate based on the lower cost of living here compared to the very large charges you would have to make for attendance at meetings in any other country apart from the UK. On one occasion one of my clients was faced with the possibility of having to pay more for my travel to a meeting than I would actually charge for my time. Needless to say we held the meeting through electronic means.

And finally …

The quality of life on the Costa del Sol overall is very good. The pace of life is much slower. Take the right, measured decisions and your future could be very happy but make the wrong decisions and you could have problems.

There are problems – they exist everywhere in the world. Life on the Costa del Sol is not perfect all the time and when problems or frustrations occur there may be times you will wonder why you came here. Suffice to say that if this happens you probably only need to return to where you came from for a few days to realise that life is better here. In all the time we have lived on the Costa del Sol we have met very few people who would even consider a return to northern Europe.

I hope this book has helped you to appreciate the positives and the negatives of living on the Costa del Sol. If it helps some readers to make the decision to move here and from the information provided their new life is easier and the settling in process is simpler – I have succeeded in what I set out to do on page one.

1

Yearly Expenditure

The table that follows is an approximation of our annual costs on the Costa del Sol. It includes what we would consider to be the essentials of a comfortable life here for two individuals who were in the fortunate position of being able to buy property without the need for a mortgage. I should also point out that it does not include the capital costs of buying new furniture, replacing computers (although the telephone costs include frequent use of the Internet and e-mail) or buying a car.

Empty columns have been included so that you can enter your own data as part of your pre-planning.

	Annual expenditure (€)	Monthly expenditure (€)
Community charges	1,800	
House insurance (contents)	240	
Car insurance and road tax	380	
Local rates	170	
Non-resident income tax	520	
Emergency medical service	200	
Health insurance		140
Electricity bills		60
Phone bills		130
Food/drink		500
Restaurants		500
Fuel (logs)	180	
Petrol		50
Prescription charges		60
	17,280	1,440
Total	20,770	

The above figure would amount to approximately £14,325 at an exchange rate of £1.00 = €1.45 (the rate at the time of writing).

2

Comparison of Food and Other Costs

(Items for which direct comparisons exist – note that where appropriate a Spanish substitute has been quoted. Exchange rate £1.00 = €1.45.)

Note also that buying English brands does not save much money – in fact they can be more expensive. Buy Spanish brands or locally produced fruit and vegetables and you will save.

Item	Unit	UK price (£)	€ equivalent	Spanish price (€)
Asparagus	1kg	7.69	11.15	2.00
Aubergines	1kg	3.59	5.20	3.59
Bananas	1kg	0.49	0.71	1.15
Beef rump	1kg	3.22	4.67	9.30
Beef mince	1kg	2.88	4.18	6.00
English bread	large	0.72	1.04	1.95
Cheddar cheese	1kg	4.15	6.01	10.56
Instant coffee	100g	1.99	2.88	2.22
Fresh chicken	2kg	4.00	5.80	2.38
Chicken breast	×2	3.83	5.55	3.53
Dry pasta	1kg	0.49	0.71	0.68
Eggs	×6	0.82	1.18	0.60
Bacon rashers	250g	1.78	2.58	2.36
Lemons	×2	0.44	0.63	0.34
Lager	2l in cans	2.84	4.11	2.30
Milk	1l	0.69	1.00	0.69
Mushrooms	0.5kg	1.20	1.74	2.48
Onions	1kg	0.49	0.71	1.29
Red peppers	×2	1.26	1.82	1.62
Orange juice	1l	0.84	1.21	1.38
Persil Auto	5kg	5.38	7.80	5.29
Pepsi	×6	2.08	3.01	2.10
Pizza	1	2.69	3.90	1.80
Rice Krispies	600g	1.99	2.88	2.53
Weetabix	24	1.16	1.68	2.79

Additional items

Items for which a direct comparison was not available at the time of writing (because my UK friends had not bought them in the supermarket!). A column has been left for you to enter the equivalent price.

Item	Price in Spain corrected to £s (£1=€1.45)	UK price
1 litre extra virgin olive oil	1.98	
Mandarins per kg	1.23	
Oranges per kg from the grower	0.41	
Strawberries per kg	0.66	
Cava (Freixenet)*	3.38	
Rioja (Faustino VII)	3.27	
White rioja (Faustino VII)	2.99	
Mineral water, 5 litres**	1.23	
Supermarket whisky	6.07	
Olives, 690g	1.23	

* Cheaper cavas are available from £2.00 in the supermarket

** Branded, Lanjaron, a mineral water locally bottled in the mountains

A selection of larger household items

- 32-inch wide-screen television (well known German brand) – £413.00

- Washing machine (supermarket special offer) – £138.00

- Tumble dryer (supermarket special offer) – £138.00

- 14-inch colour television with remote control and teletext – £54.00

- DVD player – £82.00

3

Public Holidays on the Costa del Sol

This might appear to be a strange subject to put into a book but believe me it can be very frustrating when you first move here to suddenly find everything closed just when you have run out of the necessities of life. Spain does have more public holidays than the UK and they do not all fall on dates you might expect. Expect to find banks, shops, supermarkets and other businesses closed on the following dates.

- 1 January   Ano Nuevo

- 6 January   Dia del Reys

- 28 February   Dia de Andalucia (Andalucia Day)

- 19 March   San Jose

- *   Holy Thursday

- *   Good Friday

- 1 May   Fiesta de Trabajo (Mayday)

- 24 June   San Juan

- 16 July   Dia del Carmen

- 15 August   Asuncion de la Virgen (Feast of the Assumption)

- 12 October   Dia de la Hispanidad (Columbus Day)

- 1 November   Todos los Santos (All Saints' Day)

- 6 December   Dia de la Constitucion (Constitution Day)

- 8 December   Immaculada Concepcion (Feast of the Immaculate Conception)

- 25 December   Christmas Day

* Variable dates

In addition each municipal area has its own public holiday and you will need to check this locally.

Note that if a public holiday falls on a Sunday the Monday following is not a holiday.

4 Connections by Air to Malaga and Gibraltar from the UK

Connections by air to Malaga from the UK*

London Gatwick	British Airways
	easyJet
	Excel
London Heathrow	British Airways
	Iberia
London Luton	easyJet
	Monarch
London Stansted	easyJet
Belfast	easyJet
Bristol	easyJet
Coventry**	Thomson Fly
East Midlands	easyJet
Exeter	Flybe
Edinburgh	Air Scotland
Glasgow	Air Scotland
	Excel
	Globespan (summer only)
Leeds Bradford	Jet 2
Liverpool	easyJet
Manchester	Excel
	Monarch
Newcastle	easyJet
	Excel
Southampton	Flybe

* Note that not all these services are daily and times and frequency may vary according to the season.

** This service may close down since there is conflict between Coventry Airport and Thomson

Further information can be obtained from the airlines' own Web sites or on www.lonelyplanetexchange.com/flights/cheapflights.php

Connections by air to Gibraltar from the UK

London Gatwick	British Airways
London Heathrow	British Airways
London Luton	Monarch
Manchester	Monarch (not daily)

5

International Schools on the Costa del Sol

School	Town	Telephone (dialling from the UK add 00 34)	Address
Aloha College	Nueva Andalucia	952 81 41 33	Urb El Angel Nueva Andalucia 29660 Marbella
Benalmadena International School	Benalmadena	952 56 16 66	C/Catarmanan s/n/ Nueva Torrequebrada 29630 Benalmadena Costa
Calpe College	San Pedro	952 78 14 79	Carretera de Cadiz San Pedro de Alcantara
Colegio Las Chapas (Spanish)	Elviria	952 83 16 16	Urb Las Chapas Crtra de Cadiz km1945 Elviria Marbella
English International College	Marbella	952 83 10 58	Urb Ricman Srtr de Cadiz-Malaga Marbella

School	Location	Telephone	Address
International School of Malaga	Malaga	952 20 48 10	Avda Centaurea 8 Cerrado de Calderon 29078 Malaga
St Anthony's College	Fuengirola	952 47 31 66	Apartado 119 29640 Fuengirola
St Julian's School	Marbella	952 88 81 09	Camino de Coin Mijas
Sotogrande School	Sotogrande	956 79 59 02	Apartado 15 11310 Sotogrande Cadiz
Sunny View School	Torremolinos	952 83 10 58	C/Teruel 32 Urb Cerro de Toril 29620 Torremolinos
Swan College	Marbella	952 77 32 48	Urb El Capricho s/n 29620 Marbella

Only a selection of schools which actively promote themselves can be shown here.

6 Identifying the Shop or Service

Shops

- Baker   Panaderia (bread), and Pasteleria (cakes)

- Butcher   Carniceria

- Department store   Gran almacen

- Garden centre   Jardineria

- Grocery   Tienda de ultramarinos

- Hairdresser   Peluqueria

- Ironmonger   Fereteria

- Market   Mercado

- Newsagent   Vendedor de periodicos

- Pharmacy   Farmacia

- Supermarket   Supermercado

- Tobacconist   Tabaqueria

Services

- Builder   Contratista

- Carpenter   Carpintero

- Electrician   Electricista

- Gardener   Jardinero

- Painter and decorator   Pintor

- Plumber   Plomero

Professional services

- Architect   Arquitecto

- Chiropodist   Pedicuro

- Dentist   Dentista

- Doctor   Medico

- Landscape gardener   Arquitecto de jardines

- Lawyer   Abogado

- Notary   Notario

- Vet   Veterinario

7

Costa del Sol
Golf Courses

A selection of golf courses listed from west to east along the coast:

Location	Telephone (from the UK dial 00 34)	Length (m)	Holes	Par
Alcaidesa	956 79 10 40	5,766	18	72
San Roque Club	956 61 30 30	6,494	18	72
Almenara C	956 58 20 54	6,252	18	72
Valderrama	956 79 12 00	6,234	18	72
La Canada	956 79 41 00	5,745	18	71
La Duquesa	952 89 07 25	6,054	18	72
Estepona	952 11 30 81	6,001	18	72
Los Flamingos	952 88 91 50	5,883	18	72
Monte Mayor	952 11 30 88	5,652	18	71
El Paraiso	952 88 38 35	6,131	18	71
Atalaya	952 88 28 12	6,141	18	72
Los Arqueros	952 78 46 00	5,624	18	71
La Quinta (B+C)	952 76 23 90	5,798	18	72
Los Naranjos	952 81 24 28	6,457	18	72
Cabopino	952 85 02 82	5,170	18	71
Santa Maria	952 83 03 86	5,586	18	70
La Cala	952 66 90 00	6,187	18	73
Mijas, Los Lagos	952 47 68 43	6,348	18	71
Mijas, Los Olivos	952 47 68 43	6,009	18	72
Alhaurin	952 59 59 70	6,221	18	72
Torrequebrada	952 44 27 42	5,852	18	72
Lauro (c)	952 41 27 67	5,859	18	72
El Parador	(51 01 11 20	6,204	18	72

8

Further Information

This section could be almost as long as this book itself. Over the years there have been so many books published about Spain. A quick search on the Internet will provide thousands of potential sites and titles. You, the reader of this book cannot possibly buy or indeed read all the books or access all the Web sites which are available therefore the short list below could be a useful source of further useful and detailed information on selected topics. I have not attempted to rate the information in terms of usefulness but I do have to say that the list below is only a shortlist!

Books

AA Essential Spanish Phrase Book – AA publications
Active Retirement – The *Which?* Guide
Birds of Britain and Europe – Collins Field Guide
Buying a Property in Spain – H King, How to Books
Caring for Your Pet in Spain – E and P Harrison, Santana Books
Getting a Job Abroad – R Jones, How to Books
Going to Live in Spain – H King, How to Books
Gone to Spain – T Provan, How to Books
Retire Abroad – R Jones, How to Books
The Spanish Property Guide – David Searl, Santana Books
You and the Law in Spain – D Searl, Santana Books

Newspapers

- *Sur in English* – free weekly English language newspaper covering the Costa del Sol. Large classified section. Packed with information. Published Friday

- *The Town Crier* – free weekly English language newspaper published on Mondays. Covers the Costa del Sol and Gibraltar

- *Euroweekly News* – free English language newspaper with a very good TV programme section

You will also find many glossy monthly or bi-monthly magazines free in many restaurants, bookshops and hotels.

Useful telephone numbers

Emergencies

- Costa del Sol Hospital, Marbella – 952 86 27 48

- Medical emergency – 061

- Guardia Civil (National Police) – 062

- British Consulate – 952 86 27 48

- Helicopteros Sanitarios – 952 81 18 18

Healthcare

- Helicopteros Sanitarios (emergency healthcare) – 952 81 84 96

- Medifiatc (good source of health insurance) – 952 22 75 95

- Hospital Costa del Sol, Marbella – 952 82 82 50

- Hospital Carlos Haya, Malaga – 951 03 01 00

Government offices

- INEM (Instituto Nacional de Empleo – equivalent to the job centre in the UK), Malaga head office. (local numbers in telephone directory) – 952 13 40 00

- Instituto Nacional de la Seguridad Social (social security), Malaga head office – 952 39 37 00

- Junta de Andalucia (regional government information office) – 902 50 50 50

Telephone service

- Telefonica domestic customer service – 1004

- Technical assistance for domestic customers – 1002

- Information on local businesses by category, opening hours etc. – 11888

- International information – 11825

- Spantel (a source of reduced rate phone calls similar to Oftel in the UK) – 902 18 17 18

Web site on www.spantel.es provides further information and also lets you sign up for Internet services on Spansurf.

Finding property

The Web sites listed here are of necessity a selection of the larger companies who operate the length of the Costa del Sol. In listing them I am in no way recommending these companies as a source of your dream property but rather as a source of information on what could be available for your budget. The big agents do work very closely with the developers and tend to push clients towards new property. A Web search will result in more than 150,000 sites

Local agents along the coast are a better source of resale properties and do give a more personal service. There are just too many of these to list so having chosen where you want to live you should visit the local area and select a few agents.

Mainly coastal property

- Costa del Sol Property Search – www.costadelsolpropertysearch.com

- Interealty – www.interealty.es

- Ocean Estates – www.oceanestates.com

- The Property Network – www.propertynetworkspain.com

- Royal Marbella Group – www.royalmarbellagroup.com

- Unicasa – www.unicasa.es

- Viva Estates – www.vivaestates.com

Mainly inland property

- Andalucia Country Houses – www.andalucia-country-houses.com

- Cortijo Andalucia – www.cortijo-andalucia.com

- Country Properties – www.countryproperties.net

- Rural Spain – www.ruralspain.co.uk

Furniture removal

The first advice I would give is to contact removers locally in the UK who offer an international service (search the *Yellow Pages*) and select a medium to large company with a good reputation.

If you want to use a company based on the Costa del Sol you could contact

- Bishop's Move – 00 34 956 69 81 54 (www.bishopsmove.com)

- Prima European – 00 34 952 79 02 99

- Union Jack Removals – 00 34 952 38 89 90 or UK Freephone 0800 3580289 (www.union-jack-removals.co.uk)

Transporting your pets

The following companies can organise travel for your pets from the UK to Spain and vice-versa. In addition there are also similar companies based in the UK, many of whom may probably link up with the companies listed below. The companies marked with * transport by road

- Animal Couriers* – 0 (0 44) 1483 200123

- Easypet* – 00 34 952 45 23 92

- Lady Haye – 0 (0 44) 1914 565184 (www.ladyhaye.co.uk)

- Pets Euro Travel* – 0 (0 44) 1237 472799 (www.petseurotravel.co.uk)

- V.I.Pet World – 00 34 952 41 23 53 (www.vi-pet.com)

Further information about looking after your dog in Spain

- David the Dogman (based in San Pedro) – 00 34 952 88 33 88 (www.thedogman.net)

Good Web site with many individual articles about looking after dogs and cats in Spain. Well worth visiting.

Other useful Web sites

- www.andalucia.com – general information on the Costa del Sol and many links to other useful sites including real estate agents

- www.defra.gov.uk/animal/quarantine – information about the export of pet animals

- www.dss.gov.uk – information about UK state pensions

- www.inlandrevenue.gov.uk – where to get your pension forecast or find out how to organise your tax affairs when you leave the UK

- www.ukinspain.com – main Web site of the British Embassy in Spain. The telephone number of the Consulate in Malaga appears under useful telephone numbers

- www.fsa.gov.uk – Official Web site of the Financial Services Authority for advice on financial planning

- www.naric.org.uk – Web site for NARIC which can provide information and advice on the compatibility of UK professional qualifications with working in Spain

- www.britcoun.org – The British Council can provide information on university education in the UK for people living abroad

- www.cnmv.es – For information on whether or not a financial company is registered and recognised by the Spanish authorities and the Bank of Spain

Index

WWW.NOXTAG.COM
COMPARE HOTEL
ACCOMODATION
IN ESTEPONA

WWW.CALIBOX.COM

WWW.CHEAPACCOMMODATION.COM

WWW.BESTLODGING.COM

WWW.ANDALUCIA.COM

WWW.TRIPADVISOR.COM

WWW.COSTAHOLIDAYS.COM

PROPERTY ABROAD . COM

SPANISH SCHOOLS WEBSITE

~ WWW . NABSS . ORG

OR TEL SPANISH EDUCATION ON

0207-72724

OFFICIAL ENROLMENT PRIVILEGES

* CHILDS BIRTH CERTIFICATE
        OR PASSPORT WITH OFFICIAL
SPANISH TRANSLATION

+ PROOF OF IMMUNISATION

* PROOF OF RESIDENCE - ELECTRICITY BILL,
OR PHONE BILL, OR LEASE AGREEMENT OR
PROOF OF OWNERSHIP

* PROOF OF CONVALIDATION